RIT PRESS

Romanticism in Comics: Faith, Myth, and Mood

RIT Press

RIT PRESS

Romanticism in Comics: Faith, Myth, and Mood

Nick Katsiadas

Romanticism in Comics:
Faith, Myth, and Mood

Published and distributed by:

RIT

RIT Press

90 Lomb Memorial Drive
Rochester, New York 14623
http://ritpress.rit.edu

ISBN 978-1-939125-93-4 (print)
ISBN 978-1-939125-94-1 (ebook)

Printed in the U.S.A.

Library of Congress Cataloging-in-Publication Data
Names: Katsiadas, Nick, author.
Title: Romanticism in comics : faith, myth, and mood / Nick Kastiadas.
Description: Rochester, New York : RIT Press, [2022] | Series: Comics studies monograph series ; vol 6 | Includes bibliographical references and index.
Identifiers: LCCN 2022031759 (print) | LCCN 2022031760 (ebook) | ISBN 9781939125934 (paperback) | ISBN 9781939125941 (ebook)
Subjects: LCSH: Comic books, strips, etc.—History and criticism. | Romanticism in comics. | Myth in comics. | Romanticism. | Myth in literature. | LCGFT: Literary criticism.
Classification: LCC PN6714 .K38 2022 (print) | LCC PN6714 (ebook) | DDC 741.5/9—dc23/eng/20220714
LC record available at https://lccn.loc.gov/2022031759
LC ebook record available at https://lccn.loc.gov/2022031760

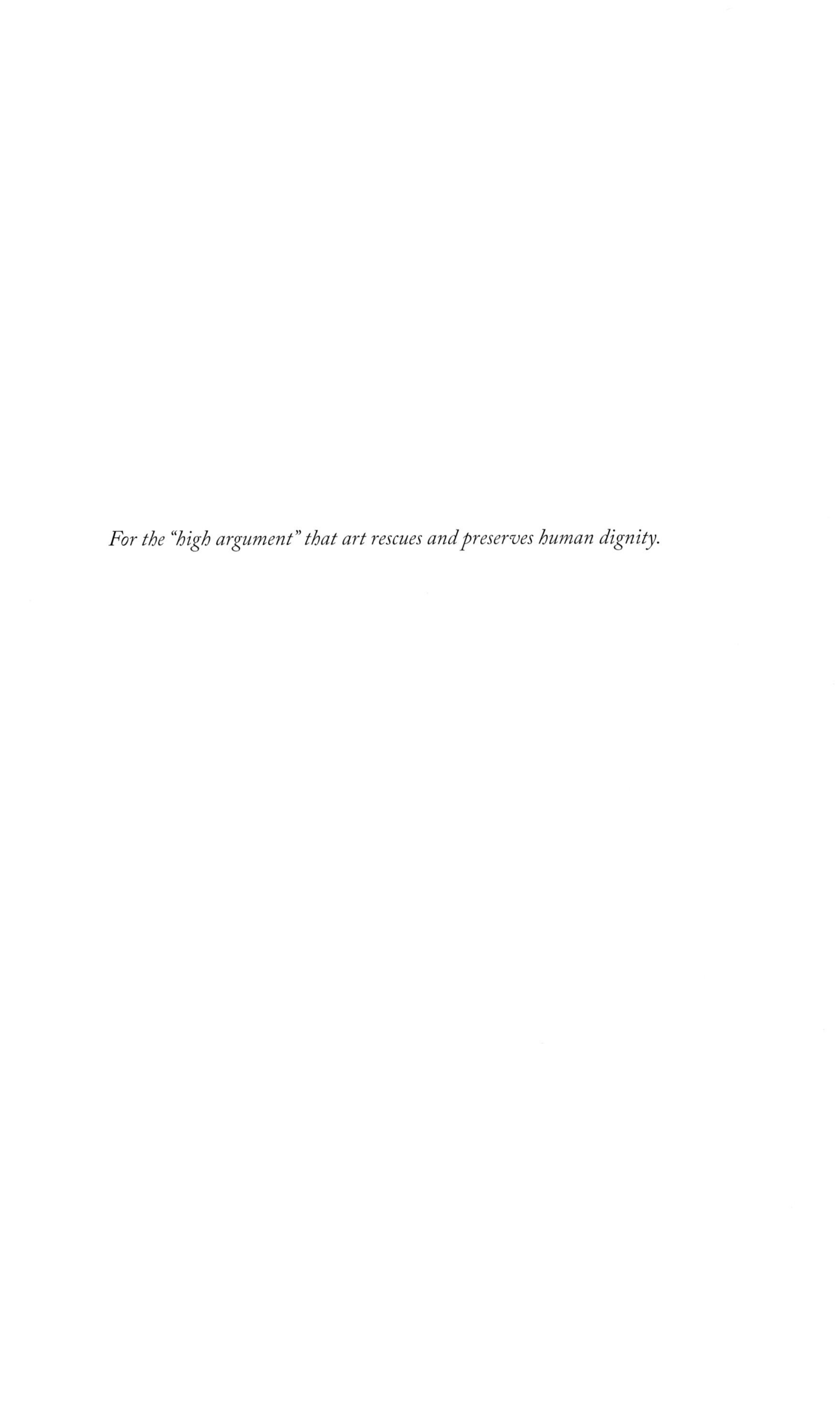

For the "high argument" that art rescues and preserves human dignity.

Comics Studies Monograph Series
Terrence R. Wandtke, Series Editor

Narrative Structure in Comics: Making Sense of Fragments
BARBARA POSTEMA

Superheroes in Crisis: Adjusting to Social Change in the 1960's and 1970's
JEFFREY K. JOHNSON

The Dark Night Returns: The Contemporary Resurgence of Crime Comics
TERRENCE R. WANDTKE

The Comics Scare Returns: The Contemporary Resurgence of Horror Comics
TERRENCE R. WANDTKE

Regarding Frames: Thinking with Comics in the Twenty-First Century
SHIAMIN KWA

Romanticism in Comics: Faith, Myth, and Mood
NICK KATSIADAS

CONTENTS

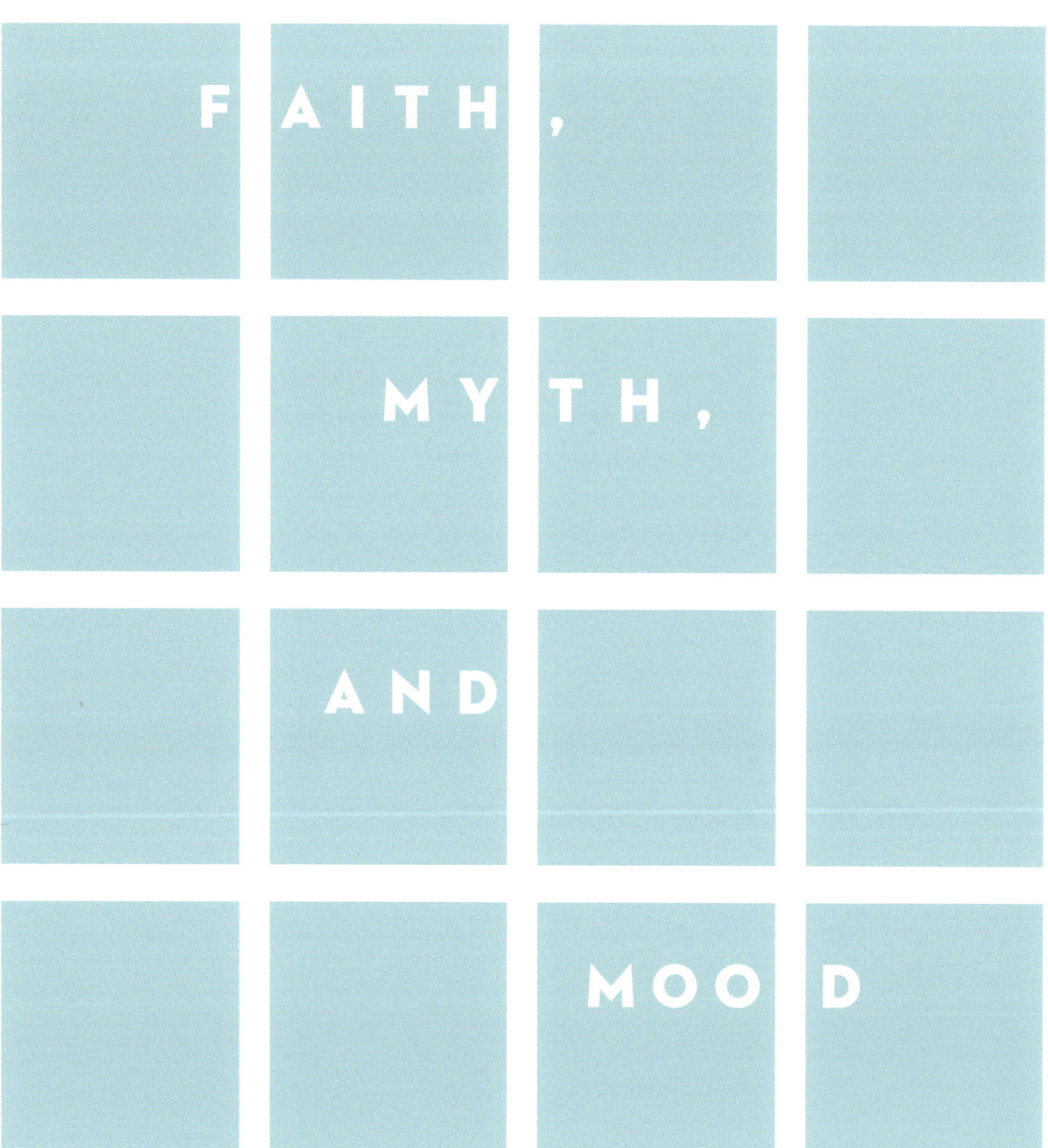
FAITH,
MYTH,
AND
MOOD

INTRODUCTION

Romanticism in Comics: Faith, Myth, and Mood

Dangers and Distortions: Opening Up Comics Scholarship

In comics studies, prevailing criticism tends to function divisively, privileging nonfiction comics over fiction and limiting comparative mythology to superhero narratives and classical and religious texts. In her *PMLA* article, for example, Hillary Chute defends the "seriousness" of nonfiction comics while, in almost the same breath, she consciously excludes fiction.[1] Since George Kovacs and C. W. Marshall's edited collections on *Classics and Comics* and *Son of Classics and Comics*, many fruitful comparative studies on comics and Greco-Roman and Norse myths have evolved while comparative studies on comics and myths in other cultures and in more recent time periods have largely been overlooked. Other conversations even put into question what critical approaches are "appropriate" for the medium. Scholar Aaron Ricker suggests that people who come to comics studies from literary backgrounds "often make the mistake of focusing on things like narrative, ignoring important [visual] things that are happening on the pages."[2] Pascal Lefèvre extends Ricker's argument and highlights the idea that "any discussion of the content or the themes of a work [without considering visual aspects] is, in fact, pointless."[3] The subtext of such criticism implies that many literary scholars approach comic books with inappropriate methodologies designed for textual, rather than visual, engagements. Such commentary intends to alert scholars to the stakes of the image-text nature of the medium, but what do we do when literary history is taking place on the pages of comics? What happens when, in Neil Gaiman's *Sandman*, William Shakespeare makes a deal with the Lord of Dreams, and in exchange for the power of dreams, he writes two plays? How are scholars supposed to read a story like Mike Carey and Peter Gross's *The Unwritten*, in which J. R. R. Tolkien, C. S. Lewis, and later writers energize modes of fantasy literature to fight a secret society trying to take over the world? And what methodology do scholars use to better understand a narrative like Alan Moore and J. H. Williams III's *Promethea*, in which a demigoddess makes appearances in literature throughout history with the goal of reconnecting humankind to the divine? If not through literary scholarship, what methods do we use to interpret these ways of representing literary history in comics?

Another problem comics studies faces is that the existing literary scholarship on comics still tends to privilege nonfiction comics over fiction, and many scholars bear conscious, almost unapologetic biases against the mainstream American comic book industry, particularly superhero comics. Chute's article claims to focus attention on "the strongest genre in the field: nonfiction comics,"[4] and to be fair, she provides shrewd insights when considering the opportunities that comics generate for exploring "historical and personal expression."[5] She demonstrates how Art Spiegelman's *Maus* (see Figure 1.1) and Joe Sacco's *Palestine* (see Figure 1.2) typify how comics are "structurally equipped to challenge dominant modes of storytelling and history writing."[6] Here, Chute capitalizes on the ways that Spiegelman and Sacco challenge dominant modes of historical representation by constructing relationships with the Holocaust and the Israel-Palestine conflict in a graphic medium. She explains how such narratives garner critical attention by offering "serious, imaginative works that [explore] social and political realities by stretching the boundaries of a historically mass medium."[7] The problem with such scholarship is not in the ways that it reads nonfiction comics as strong narratives but in how it continues to capitalize on ideas that the "dominant" and "most important graphic narratives" are nonfiction works that "portray torture and massacre in a complex formal mode that does not turn away from

Fig. 1.1
The cover art for Art Spiegelman's *Maus*. Image courtesy of Penguin Random House LLC.

Fig. 1.2
The cover art for Joe Sacco's *Palestine*. Copyright © Joe Sacco. Courtesy of Fantagraphics Books. (www.fantagraphics.com).

or mitigate trauma."[8] Critical opportunities arise with her use of the terms "dominant," "most important," and how she explains that it is "not a coincidence" that narratives of trauma are "waking up literary critics."[9]

For Chute, narrative strength is determined by the ways nonfiction artists form relationships with "vicious historical realities."[10] What is missing from this scope is the greater spectrum of historical experience from which artists draw and how the medium offers a greater range of genres beyond nonfiction, where artists both challenge dominant modes of storytelling and represent history in equally important ways. Further, Chute consciously excludes historical representation in mainstream titles when providing an abbreviated history of the medium. She writes, "I offer a context for American work but do not emphasize the development of the commercial comic-book industry, which is dominated by two superhero-focused publishers, Marvel and DC."[11] Chute's dismissal of the mainstream American comic book industry offers a glimpse into deep-seated biases against mass culture forms of media in critical discourse, and such stances create opportunities to open up conversations about historical representation in comics and popular fiction, in general.

The importance of opening up historical inquiry to mainstream comic book titles rests in what Ben Saunders addresses as threatening "Divisions in Comics Scholarship" in his letter to the editor in the *PMLA* journal. Saunders's letter responds to Chute's claims that nonfiction is the most important genre. He writes, "Dangers and distortions threaten when we allow generic divisions to shape our critical narratives."[12] Here he addresses how even though Chute's goal is to "treat comics as a medium—not as a lowbrow genre,"[13] she shapes a hierarchy between genres—between highbrow (nonfiction) and lowbrow (mainstream fiction). It is no secret: We can accept Chute's stance that nonfiction comics have a large presence within university studies and garner much critical attention. Saunders does not doubt this claim, nor does he doubt that nonfiction is a strong genre. What he does is caution the field against forming separate canons and being "divided from within":[14]

> Old-fashioned and politically divisive arguments about high culture versus low culture, or fine art versus commercial art, have a disturbing tendency to reassert themselves along generic lines. Despite the best efforts of literary theorists to deconstruct such aesthetic hierarchies, they prove remarkably resilient. Indeed, with almost tragic irony, these hierarchies frequently reproduce themselves in the criticism of art forms traditionally regarded as debased.[15]

Saunders calls for comics studies scholars to learn from the critical histories of other fields and to avoid the limitations and exclusions that canon formations create if they want the discipline to survive and thrive. Saunders concludes his letter to Chute by capitalizing on this point: "We require such skepticism regarding academic canons from our graduate students in literary studies, film studies, and art history, after all. The future of comics studies will surely require no less of us."[16] This is a stance with which everyone can get on board. The importance of Chute and Saunders's exchange against the backdrop of conversations about "appropriate" approaches to comics cannot be overstated, and this book takes advantage of it.

First, Saunders's warning encourages us to keep critical lines of inquiry open to all genres that the medium offers and to facilitate the field's growth when treating the medium along generic lines. This book uses this premise and opens up the field by arguing that if we can use certain methodologies to glean meaning from historical representation in nonfiction, then we can use similar methodologies to glean meaning from historical representation in mainstream fiction. Second, although Chute privileges nonfiction and representations of trauma, her framework is helpful in reading how mainstream comic book artists construct relationships with history, and I open up her framework to a greater spectrum of historical experience that comic book artists represent—namely, how artists construct relationships with literary traditions. The ways that artists represent and construct relationships with literary history leads to my third point: We can extend Saunders's and Chute's frameworks to mainstream titles and demonstrate instances where it is appropriate to approach comics with literary-critical methodologies. If we avoid constructing boundaries along generic and critical lines, we can open the field to greater understandings of the medium's literary history and the medium's place in larger, historically distinct discourses.

This book examines historical representation in titles from the Modern Age[17] of comics: Gaiman's *Sandman*, Moore and Williams's *Promethea*, and Carey and Gross's *The Unwritten*.[18] These titles, I argue, can be better understood as occupying spaces between mainstream fiction and historically based nonfiction and autobiography. The key to this understanding rests in remaining open to insights from literary criticism. I take Chute's perspectives of the "productively self-aware" artist of nonfiction[19] and extend them to artists who consciously recreate literary history. In Chute's words, "Graphic narrative suggests that historical accuracy is not the opposite of creative invention,"[20] and this idea is helpful in reading how Gaiman, Moore and Williams, and Carey and Gross invent mythologies and use them to construct not only narrative relationships but also personal relationships with literary history.

Transforming Literary History into Myth in Comics

Conversations about comic book genres, historical representation, and literary history do not need to remain closed, static, and exclusive; they can, and should, be open, porous, and interstitial. Such a critical step is possible by considering the different ways that Gaiman, Moore and Williams, and Carey and Gross construct historical narratives in which literature is directly linked to the totality of human integrity and experience. Chute's framework suggests that artists reimagine the past in order to construct meaningful relationships with it, and these artists reimagine and reconstruct relationships with literary history on a few narrative levels. They construct relationships between new characters in their stories and characters and works of the literary past; these relationships indicate the the ways in which the artists construct individual relationships with literary traditions; and both of these relationships suggest that the comics medium represents a greater spectrum of emotional experience within, beyond "vicious historical realities." *Sandman*, *Promethea,* and *The Unwritten* are series in which the artists invent mythologies with value systems for reading human integrity's connection to literature. In their myths, these systems encourage readers to understand the relationships between human history, modernity, and the purpose and function of imaginative literature. The artists transform literary history into totalizing mythological narratives, and myth provides the artists an imaginative vehicle to reinterpret and re-present literary history in distinct ways. The irony is that the artists become a part of the history that they reinterpret with personal myths.

Historical representation becomes an interpretive act for Gaiman, Moore and Williams, and Carey and Gross, and mythology becomes their interpretive vehicle in all three series. Each mythology constructs human history as being contingent on the imaginative storytelling for which mythical deities are responsible. In *Sandman*, for instance, Gaiman builds the imaginary world of The Dreaming, a space/place that connects all human consciousness into one shared dream-world. The title character, Morpheus, obsesses over his responsibilities to maintain this realm, and the drama of the story unfolds as he learns what it is like to be human. One way that he fulfills his duties is by creating new stories for humankind to tell and gifting them to authors in the form of dreams. In *Sandman*, dreams are commensurate with stories, and throughout human history, authors become extensions of Morpheus's power and will to maintain the integrity of human consciousness. The logic is that imaginative literature helps humankind understand the world and how to live in it. In a similar way, Moore and Williams build the imaginary realm of The Immateria, a space/place from which all imaginative creativity emanates. This realm's patron, Promethea, wields imaginative, creative powers that reconnect humankind to divine energies. The story follows how Promethea must learn how to use these energies and maintain humankind's connections to them, and she does so by traveling through metaphysical worlds, including the Kabbalist Tree of Life and a deck of tarot cards. Carey and Gross create a mythology in which a metaphysical white whale named Leviathan develops human integrity by energizing storytelling throughout history. Throughout the narrative, a group of characters—Tom Taylor, Lizzie Hexam, and Richard Savoy—learn how to use stories in order to protect Leviathan from historical forces of tyranny and oppression. The logic is that storytelling drives human history, and powerful groups of people attempt to make humankind submit to their lies—to their stories. The common factors in these three titles are that imaginative fiction becomes an extension of benevolent creative energies, and mythical figures become vehicles through which the artists reinterpret the history of storytelling as a force benefitting humankind. A closer reading of the narratives suggests that all three mythologies share one broader idea: faith in imaginative creativity's potential to elevate humankind's state of being.

In *Sandman*, *Promethea*, and *The Unwritten*, the artists construct historical models that elevate ideas about the ways imaginative storytelling is a force that sets and sustains guidance for human understandings of reality. The narratives' logic follows how imaginative stories are pedagogical and affective; the integrity of human history is contingent on the lessons found in stories and the affective experiences that they elicit. Moreover, a distinct irony is at play in these titles, where fiction meets nonfiction. The artists are engaged in acts of storytelling while using invented myths to ascribe redeeming values to acts of storytelling throughout history. The artists become a part of their own myths on formal, self-reflexive levels. They are (to use Chute's words) "productively self-aware" artists. They are completely aware of this irony and exert ownership of it.

The formal aesthetics of consciously re-presenting literary history satisfy the demands of current scholarly conversations to consider what is happening, visually, on the pages of comics and how comic book artists are aware of "how they 'materialize' history."[21] Literary history is happening on the pages of *Sandman*, *Promethea*, and *The Unwritten*, and it is logical to turn to literary-critical histories to better understand how the artists represent it. The formal-aesthetic intersections between fiction and nonfiction come to the fore in the ways that the artists ironically create stories about the virtues of creating stories. A specular function of the artists is at play in each series: from visibly representing themselves in panels (as we see in *Promethea*[22]) to visible images of literary texts within texts that reflect on the function of texts. The artists' invented myths complement the artists' personal ideas about imaginative creativity and senses of responsibility to create stories. The narrative associations with literary history function on at least two levels. On one, they create opportunities for their characters to interact with what is constructed as their literary ancestors, including historically based authors such as Rudyard Kipling, G. K. Chesterton, and Shakespeare; preexisting literary characters such as Queen Titania, King Auberon, Moby Dick, and Frankenstein's Creature; and preexisting imaginary worlds such as Wonderland, Narnia, and Middle-earth. The artists create narrative parallels between their stories and preexisting literature through such interactions, indicating sources that energize their creativity.

On another level, what these interactions signal—and is missing from much scholarship dedicated to the titles—is an intense self-reflexivity: The artists consciously connect the storytelling with which they are engaged to the ideals of their myths. Such a reading creates critical opportunities both to consider dimensions of nonfiction in mainstream fiction and to discuss how artists reinterpret, recreate, and construct personal relationships with literary history in ways that intersect with creative processes within literary antecedents.

It is important to the field of comics studies that we reveal intersections between nonfiction and mainstream fiction so that we may better understand genre, creative impetus, and comics' greater literary history. One problem that we meet when pursuing a greater literary history of comics, however, is in how prevailing criticism tends to limit *Sandman*, *Promethea*, and *The Unwritten* to postmodern literary history. Many critics read the artists' creative impetus and formal structures in terms of postmodern pastiche, adaptation, intertextuality, and metafiction. Peter Wilkins, for example, identifies how Carey and Gross's *The Unwritten* incorporates elements from preexisting stories in a "metafictional science fiction" mode of narration.[23] Similarly, Cyril Camus examines postmodern commonalities in Gaiman's and Moore's work: "[S]ome features are also common to both, from their extended practice of integrative fiction or metafiction to their pervasive concern with mythology, both as mere intertext and as a model for their brand of fantasy."[24] Roderick McGillis also explores how "Moore's work updates its source material in what we might call a postmodern dance of selves."[25] The subtext of such criticism typifies how critics understand form and creative process in terms of late-twentieth and twenty-first century creative practices. The aesthetics of historical representation in these works, however, suggest that contemporary art is not as uniform as criticism assumes it to be. An alternative to the postmodern orientation is to examine historical representation, genre, and the artists' creative process. The process of transforming literary history into myth suggests distinct and distinctly different intersections between comics and literary history. It suggests that we find intersections between the commercial comic book industry and literature of the Romantic period.[26] The question, therefore, becomes, are artists who use personal myths as vehicles to express their faith in imaginative creativity supposed to be any less Romantic because they weren't born in the nineteenth century?

Romantic Aesthetics in Comics

It would be inaccurate to assume that narrative practices in Gaiman's *Sandman*, Moore and Williams's *Promethea*, and Carey and Gross's *The Unwritten* descend from or intersect with literary Romanticism in some uniform way. After all, Romanticism is as diverse as it is consensual, and these artists connect with distinctly different literary traditions that have roots in Romanticism. The benefit of turning to the Romantic period to better understand *Sandman*, *Promethea,* and *The Unwritten* is that we bring new insights to preexisting scholarship in both Romantic and comics studies. For example, many scholars believe that the image-text nature and

The Divine Image.

To Mercy Pity Peace and Love.
All pray in their distrefs:
And to these virtues of delight
Return their thankfulnefs.

For Mercy Pity Peace and Love,
Is God our father dear:
And Mercy Pity Peace and Love,
Is Man his child and care.

For Mercy has a human heart
Pity, a human face:
And Love, the human form divine,
And Peace, the human drefs.

Then every man of every clime,
That prays in his distrefs,
Prays to the human form divine
Love Mercy Pity Peace.

And all must love the human form,
In heathen, turk or jew,
Where Mercy, Love & Pity dwell
There God is dwelling too.

Fig. 1.3
An example of William Blake's illuminated poetry, titled "The Divine Image," from *The Songs of Innocence and Experience*. Image 14 from William Blake, *The Songs of Innocence and of Experience, Shewing the Two Contrary States of the Human Soul* (London, W. Blake, 1794). Library of Congress, Lessing J. Rosenwald Collection, https://www.loc.gov/item/48031329/.

formal characteristics of comics were developed during the Romantic period. Jack Stillinger and Deidre Lynch discuss the ways that the image-text nature of William Blake's illuminated manuscripts have a "marked influence" on creative processes in contemporary comics (see Figure 1.3).[27] David Kunzle also acknowledges how it may "reasonably be said" that Rodolphe Töpffer, a nineteenth-century Genevan schoolmaster, revolutionized the "speed" at which we tell stories in sequence.[28] Chute addresses how such critical moves make "claims in the name of popular culture or in the rich tradition of word-and-image inquiry."[29] She also explains that these moves are "obvious"—and they are. But what is less obvious and missing from current conversations is that comparing creative process reveals hitherto unsuspected connections between comics, nineteenth-century literary history, and the larger discourse of the history of emotions. The importance in exploring these connections is in the ways that comics become part of larger, historically distinct discourses in our contemporary moment—not a discursive history of trauma, as with Chute's framework, but what we will see as a discursive history of *paranoia*.

First, however, we need a framework with which to approach creative process, and genre is a great place to start. *Sandman*, *Promethea*, and *The Unwritten* are fruitful for comparative mythology because, like their Romantic literary ancestors, these comic book

Fig. 1.4
The figure Los, as he appears in *The Book of Urizen*. Image 22 from William Blake, *The Book of Urizen* (Lambeth: Printed by W. Blake, 1815). Library of Congress, Lessing J. Rosenwald Collection, https://www.loc.gov/item/49034226/.

artists absorb literary history into myths that venerate the human imagination and creativity. Within Blake's *Four Zoas*, for example, the mythical figure Urthona represents the artist's ideas about imagination and creativity, and he is one of four beings divided from Albion, the primordial man. The logic is that these divine emanations have "fallen into division" among humankind; they are innate within every individual but in "fallen" forms, such as Urthona's appearance as Los (see Figure 1.4). Likewise, Percy Bysshe Shelley, in *Prometheus Unbound*, uses the figure Prometheus as a vehicle to represent personal ideas about the imagination's power to liberate humankind. In this work, the titan's release from his imprisonment on Caucasus dramatizes Shelley's ideas about the modern poet's (i.e., his own) sense of imaginative freedom and the "spirit of the age." By comparison, Gaiman, Moore and Williams, and Carey and Gross also create mythologies that dramatize ideas venerating the powers of imagination and creativity: Morpheus, Promethea, and Leviathan become vehicles to represent these ideas. Even more important, like Blake and Shelley, the comic book artists reflexively function within the histories of imagination and creativity that they recreate: The artists invent *and* become a part of the history that their myths convey. Gaiman is "writing a dream"; Moore and Williams are wielding the "magical" powers of storytelling; and Carey and Gross are "growing" a story. This comparative approach between comics and Romantic myths provides at least three generative insights to prevailing criticism, both in comics and Romantic studies: Comics can occupy spaces between nonfiction and fiction; comics have a greater literary history; and comics have a greater spectrum of formal aesthetics at play, which can help us better understand literary history. Where and when these aesthetics develop, what historical conditions energize them; how they persist in our contemporary moment; and what lasting influences aesthetics have on artistic creativity are all generative questions for comics studies and studies in Romanticism. Answers to these questions can be found in slow and patient methods of reading genre in terms of historical representation and literary ancestors.

We meet another two difficulties, however, when approaching comics from the perspective of Romantic mythology and literary history: skepticism in the field to use literary-historical approaches and the critical tendency to limit comparative mythology to comics and classical mythology. Aaron Meskin's ideas about comics' artistic ancestors help us approach both issues. Meskin includes literature among comics' ancestors, but he also cedes that each title's ancestors vary and all comics do not require the same ancestors. For instance, some comics do not contain words: "That is, there are wordless comics (sometimes called 'mute' or 'pantomime' comics), and these do not seem to meet a necessary minimal condition" for having literary ancestors.[30] When literary elements are present, however, we may "appropriately appreciate the literary aspects…in light of the norms and styles and concerns that attach to literature."[31] We can hold not only appropriate but important conversations about the ways that literary elements function in comics, and we can take Meskin's ideas about literary ancestors a step further with *Sandman*, *Promethea*, and *The Unwritten* by consulting larger critical histories attached to genre conventions of myth and the creative process of reimagining literary history with invented myth.

Surely as Meskin argues that comics have multiple artistic ancestors, they also have multiple mythological ancestors, but recent studies in comparative mythology tend to be myopic in examining superhero comics' relationships with classical myths and religious texts. The popular idea of superheroes as a "modern mythology" typically does not venture outside these limits.[32] Even discussions that reject the idea that comics are a "modern mythology" tend to limit their thinking about comparative engagements with ancient myths.[33] Certainly, some forms of myth-making are not considered within the critical discourse, and Romantic myth-making is one of several.[34] My point is that stark contrasts exist between mythologies in different time periods and in different spaces/places. The contrast between classical and Romantic mythologies rests in nineteenth-century revisions of the powers of myths: The Romantics developed metaphysical systems that energized ways of thinking about imagination and creativity, and their ways of thinking about literature and the arts persisted up through the late nineteenth century and into the twentieth and twenty-first centuries.

Despite the current myopia in comparative mythology and comics, the critical foundations are useful for better understanding not only Romanticism's importance to comics studies but also comics' importance to Romantic studies. Kyle Johnson, for example, makes the case that comics studies scholars build interpretive systems that can be helpful to read the literary past, particularly classical texts.[35] He demonstrates how Thierry Groensteen's methods for reading narrative sequence in comics reveal narrative sequence in ekphrasis[36] in Homer's *Iliad*. He applies this methodology to Homer's description of the Shield of Achilles and brings new insights into the creative process. He concludes that ekphrasis creates an organization of visuals that is sequential and coordinated according to its poetics, such as theme, narrative progression, image, and meter.[37] Johnson's focus on classical texts can serve as a critical model for how comics studies can help us reread and better understand Romanticism's legacy in twentieth- and twenty-first-century art forms. Chute's framework for reading historical representation in comics can help us better understand a greater literary history and legacy of Romanticism up through our contemporary moment than hitherto suspected. These new, generative understandings are possible when we diachronically read historical representation and the creative process of myth-making in *Sandman*, *Promethea*, and *The Unwritten*.

Understanding the Romantic state of mind becomes key when reading comics creativity as continuing Romantic legacies. Isaiah Berlin's discussion of this state of mind provides insight into the movement's lasting effects on creativity and our ways of thinking about imagination and creativity. Berlin explains that the Romantic period "deeply influenced" human thought and behavior in the nineteenth and twentieth centuries.[38] He describes how the late eighteenth and early nineteenth century mark a shift in the Western state of mind, and he suggests that we can identify this shift in the dominant creative patterns of the time. These patterns, in other words, reveal a consensus of thought: "The history not only of thought, but of consciousness, opinion, action too, of morals, politics, aesthetics, is to a large degree a history of dominant models."[39] The Romantic state of mind, he argues, gradually developed from the mid-eighteenth century onward as a reaction against the Enlightenment state of mind. The Enlightenment was dominated by ideas about attaining "some kind of rational order, in which tragedy, vice and stupidity… can at last be avoided by the use of carefully acquired information and the application to it of universally intelligible reason."[40] Such Enlightenment models posit how we will only discover truths about the universe and liberate ourselves from folly, suffering, and destruction by committing to empirical science, reason, and logic.

Berlin goes on to discuss how Romantic writers attacked Enlightenment ideas about the "absolute knowledge" that awaits discovery in at least two ways:

> [W]hat the romantic movement proclaimed, may be summarised [*sic*] under two heads. One of these…is the indomitable will: not knowledge of values, but their creation, is what men achieve. You create values, you create goals, you create ends, and in the end you create your own vision of the universe, exactly as artists create works of art…
>
> The second proposition—connected with the first—is that there is no structure of things. There is no pattern to which you must adapt yourself. There is only, if not the flow, the endless self-creativity of the universe.[41]

Romantic artists venerated acts of creativity and the power of the human will within their work, not acts of discovery. The idea that humankind wills itself to create develops in this period at the same time as artists become elevated in the human imagination as humanity's heroes. This is when the Romantic hero emerges as a dominant figure within creative patterns, and this figure becomes integral to authors' ways of conveying personal ideas about artistic responsibility. Berlin suggests that these patterns affected humankind's ways of thinking about the world and the artist's place within it, and I propose that the work of Neil Gaiman, Alan Moore and J. H. Williams III, and Mike Carey and Peter Gross become extensions of Romantic patterns of creativity.

Many scholars concur that Romantic ideas about artistic creativity and responsibility became dominant patterns of the nineteenth century that have had lasting effects. M. H. Abrams, for instance, suggests that Romantic "thinkers gave literature and the arts a prominent...place in their metaphysical systems."[42] Ideas about a larger system of human creativity take an enormous hold during the Romantic period, and the figure of the heroic poet ascends as a dominant pattern. Within literary works, artistic figures become mythical figures and take pride of place as dedicating—and sacrificing—their lives to ideals of creating and sustaining human integrity through what Friedrich Schiller calls the "aesthetic education of man."[43] Ideas about creativity and the role of art in one's education are validated *as valuable* during the Romantic period, and they are two of its most important legacies. Within Romantic myths, creativity becomes the driving force of history, art becomes a secular religion of modernity, and we find these ideas energizing artistic creativity from the late eighteenth century through the nineteenth century, and right up through our contemporary moment—in *Sandman*, *Promethea*, and *The Unwritten*.

Walking Comics Backwards: Literary Inheritance and the History of Emotions

Michael Saler's ideas about ongoing literary projects create space in comics studies to better understand how artists act as mediators of the Romantic tradition. These ideas are also a good place to start walking comics backwards from the twenty-first century. Saler traces contemporary imaginative fiction, particularly science fiction and fantasy, to early twentieth-century literary traditions. He argues that many artists who functioned within these traditions became united in a literary project to compensate for a "disenchanted" world.[44] This idea, made famous by Max Weber in 1919, conveys a collective state of mind in which wonder, mystery, traditional beliefs, and "stable"[45] ways of understanding the world begin to disappear or, at best, lose influence. He chiefly isolates the work of three literary figures—J. R. R. Tolkien, H. P. Lovecraft, and Sir Arthur Conan Doyle—to advance the argument that artists sought to compensate for this state of mind with imaginative works. Saler extends this argument to mainstream comic books, suggesting that they act as allies in the project to "reenchant" the world: "[The 1960s] was notable for the emergence of impassioned fan communities that immersed themselves in the imaginary worlds of J. R. R. Tolkien's *The Lord of the Rings*, Robert E. Howard's Conan the Barbarian, the Marvel Comics' Universe and the DC 'Multiverse.'"[46] Such artists, he observes, committed to artistic ideals about providing solutions for spiritual problems arising from an increasingly secular, reason-based culture. Joshua Landy and Saler discuss this turn to secular reason as creating a "God-shaped void" for which artists sought to compensate with imaginative creativity.[47]

The goal of the project to "reenchant the world" was to invite readers into imaginary spaces in an effort to restore wonder, mystery, and meaning in a disenchanted modernity. Saler suggests that to achieve this goal, artists "freed [themselves] from the religious and utilitarian strictures of [Samuel Taylor] Coleridge's era," or the Romantic era.[48] This liberation from religious and utilitarian strictures may be, but they are not as confining as they seem to be. The secular and the sacred often meet in nineteenth-century literature, and comics can help us better understand how these intersections persist within artistic creativity into the twentieth and twenty-first centuries. Moreover, this framework suggests that *Sandman*, *Promethea*, and *The Unwritten* help us better understand not only comics history but also Romantic literary history. In short, comics can help us better understand literature. It may not be a popular approach of interpretation in critical discourse, but it is a concrete one grounded in exploring the presence of literary elements within comics and drawing from literary-critical history to read such elements.

We can expand on existing comics scholarship grounded in the Romantic period by opening up Saler's ideas about the project of reenchantment to Romanticism and expanding on his comments about comics. William Buckler's research helps us make such a critical step. Where Saler argues that early twentieth-century artists freed themselves from Romanticism, Buckler helps us better understand how a secular, Romantic "faith" in imaginative letters found its way into twentieth- and twenty-first-century literature. I propose that we can also extend this perspective to comics if we remain open to insights from critical histories outside of comics scholarship. Buckler describes a "poetic faith that, allowing for the secularization and deflation of language, persists right through [W. B.] Yeats, [T. S.] Eliot, [Wallace] Stevens, and [Robert] Lowell as the archetypal Romantic faith."[49] The process of secularizing inherited religious experiences in order to energize the human imagination and regenerate a relationship with the sacred world through art was central to nineteenth-century Romanticism's faith in imaginative creativity. Expressions of this faith continued to persist in artistic creativity up through the nineteenth and twentieth centuries—in literary traditions that appear in *The Unwritten*, *Promethea*, and *Sandman*. Buckler's framework suggests that these comic book series convey similar concerns, and each chapter in this book provides evidence of a logical chronology in the persistence of Romantic faith: Gaiman, Moore and Williams, and Carey and Gross not only recall and intersect with the Romantic process of using myth to elevate creativity as energizing human integrity and driving human history, but they also connect their narratives to authors whose works are directly and indirectly influenced by Romanticism. We are encountering a diachronic literary history of Romanticism in comics.

A diachronic framework allows us to identify the persistence of Romanticism in comics in the ways that artists invent mythologies that highlight historically-based imaginative traditions. These traditions include historically-based artists of fantasy literature, such as G. K. Chesterton in *Sandman* and J. R. R. Tolkien, C. S. Lewis, and the Inkling literary circle within *The Unwritten*, and they also include metaphysical systems that we find in occult movements, such as Christian Kabbalist ways of thinking about imagination and creativity that we find in *Promethea*. Each series connects with early twentieth-century literary traditions, and although each tradition might convey different ideas about the world and how to live in it, they all share one broader idea: The urgency to create imaginative literature throughout human history. The Romantics energized this idea, and the Romantic urgency for imaginative creativity persists in *Sandman*, *Promethea*, and *The Unwritten*. It is seen in the ways that the narratives evaluate historical tensions and posit how resolutions must be achieved within literary realms. Berlin's, Saler's, and Buckler's frameworks suggest that Gaiman, Moore and Williams, and Carey and Gross commit to the rules that their mythologies create: contributing to an ongoing historical process of creating art that energizes humankind's state of being.

The idea that history is a system of human creativity is a general consensus in Romantic, Victorian, and Modernist literature, and it is also a general consensus in much contemporary creativity, including *Sandman*, *Promethea*, and *The Unwritten*. This way of thinking about creativity suggests that human integrity is contingent on the literary creativity that individuals inherit and engage. Art, in the Romantic frame of mind, becomes an aesthetic space in which individuals explore systems of historical evolution while also exploring their function within these systems.

Abrams demonstrates how the Romantics energized this idea of literary inheritance. He writes, "The several decades beginning with the 1790s constituted a genuine epoch in intellectual and cultural history; not, however, by absolute innovation but by a return to a mode of hereditary wisdom which was redefined, expanded, and applied to the emerging world."[50] Here, Abrams explains how many Romantic writers use literature to express commitments to restore humankind's awareness of inheriting wisdom within larger historical processes. The aesthetic space becomes a means for self-expression, and in comics, artists use aesthetic spaces to express similar ideas about literary inheritance and engagement as being contingent on human integrity.

Gaiman, Moore and Williams, and Carey and Gross intersect with Romantic ideas about literary creativity and inheritance, and Chute's framework helps us focus historical representations—in image and in text—as forms of self-expression. This framework also brings this book into the fold of preexisting genre studies that are oriented toward historical representations of narrative inheritance in nonfiction comics. James Young, for example, argues that Art Spiegelman's *Maus* emerges from a post-World War II generation of Holocaust survivors who inherit historical narratives. He writes,

> *Maus* also suggests itself as a model for what I would like to call "received history"…This postwar generation, after all, cannot remember the Holocaust as it actually occurred. All they remember, all they know of the Holocaust, is what the victims have passed down to them in their diaries, what the survivors have remembered to them in their memoirs. They remember not actual events but the countless histories, novels, and poems of the Holocaust they have read, the photographs, movies, and video testimonies they have seen over the years. They remember long days and nights in the company of survivors, listening to their harrowing tales, until their lives, loves, and losses seemed grafted indelibly onto their own life stories.[51]

Here, Young discusses how Spiegelman highlights the process of inheriting his father Vladek's Holocaust narrative, and he argues that not only does he inherit a historical narrative but also the trauma attached to the narrative. He suggests that representing such inheritances is a consensual creative pattern of this postwar generation. Vladek's story, in other words, is passed to Art Spiegelman, and the transference, not only of one generation's historical experience but also their emotional experience, is brought to the foreground. If we borrow Young's framework to read representations of narrative inheritance, we can open new lines of historical inquiry in mainstream comics to other emotional experiences attached to narratives.

We need to remain open to the idea that comics artists are not limited to representing the inheritance of nonfiction narratives energized by trauma, nor do historical narratives representing trauma take pride of place in narrative complexity or strength. If we combine

Young's method to read narrative inheritance with Romantic notions of inherited wisdom, we can better understand the literary histories with which Gaiman, Moore and Williams, and Carey and Gross construct relationships, and we can better understand the paranoia attached to those literary histories. In doing so, we shift attention to a greater spectrum of emotions represented in comics, and we can shift attention in the current discourses of *Sandman*, *Promethea*, and *The Unwritten*—from reading literary presences as postmodern metafiction or pastiche to reading literary presences as literary inheritances. The artists reimagine literary history within invented myths, and these myths foreground ideas about artists inheriting creative responsibilities to function within larger historical systems of storytelling.

Comics studies suggest that writers and visual artists work together to advance narrative, and Chute's ideas about the productively self-aware artist suggest that the ideas about history that narratives foreground rebound on the artists. This framework suggests that Gaiman, Moore and Williams, and Carey and Gross signal an awareness of inheriting responsibilities to the histories of storytelling that they recreate. This sense of responsibility does not indicate an inheritance of trauma but, rather, paranoia: Paranoia emerges in *Sandman*, *Promethea*, and *The Unwritten* in the ways that the artists *imagine* a historical urgency to create art. Whether their historical assessments are accurate does not determine whether the narratives contain paranoid paradigms. What determines paranoia is their anxious way of interpreting history as dependent on the artistic productivity with which they are engaged; just like their Romantic ancestors, this paranoia is dramatized by personal myths.

Genre becomes key for reading *Sandman*, *Promethea*, and *The Unwritten* as paranoid narratives. Their artists take initiatives to connect their creativity to a greater literary inheritance through myth, and how the Romantics understood the role of art—myth, in particular—is important for discussing paranoia as an inherited historical experience in comics. Many Romantic writers saw myth as having a distinct purpose and function to create new understandings of reality and to push human progress forward. Berlin writes, "Myths were ways in which human beings expressed their sense of the ineffable, inexpressible mysteries of nature, and there was no other way in which it could be expressed...Myths conveyed this mystery in artistic images and artistic symbols, which, without words, managed to connect man with the mysteries of nature. This, roughly speaking, was the doctrine."[52] Here, Berlin suggests how myth provided a narrative versatility and freedom to represent what "could be expressed only symbolically and could not be expressed literally."[53] The idea that literature, particularly mythology, connects man to primal powers became energized during the Romantic period, and literary creativity itself was "converted into rich sources of mythology" during this time.[54] Mythical figures become vehicles for the artist's personal ideas about art. Berlin writes of such figures: "This view of great images dominating mankind—of dark forces, of the unconscious, of the importance of the inexpressible and the necessity of discounting it and allowing for it—spreads into every sphere of human activity."[55] The Romantics used myth to construct literature as an extension of ineffable creative powers driving human history, and authors become a part of this history by *creating art about the power of art.* These "great images" of artists exerting power over humankind spread into every sphere of artistic creativity in the nineteenth century, and as we will see, they maintain an afterlife in our historical moment, including within comics creativity.

Paranoia becomes legible in artistic figures that commit to guarding humankind against forces outside of their control through artistic creativity, and Romantic criticism provides critical frameworks for reading Gaiman's, Moore and Williams's, and Carey and Gross's figures in this way. Thomas Pfau, for instance, encourages scholars to read different manifestations of Romantic paranoia in popular culture. He writes,

> [P]opular culture of the past two decades has been filled with conspiratorial narratives—many of them revolving around late capitalism's transnational corporations scheming to conceal the presence of alien organisms within the community of the "human." In an update on earlier, strictly political conspiracies… popular cinematic culture of the 1980s and 1990s dramatizes paranoia as a condition experienced by individuals or groups who feel their very status as "human" to be under siege. From Ridley Scott's *Alien* films to James Cameron's *The Terminator* bonanza, from *Blade Runner* to *X-Men* and *The X-Files*… conspiracies shrewdly conceived and robotically executed by abstract forces of global capital ultimately target for elimination the very idea of our "essential" humanity.[56]

Here, Pfau argues that formal aesthetics of paranoia are legible in our contemporary moment in the ways artists create narratives that *imagine* humankind coming under pressures of the nonhuman and losing a "fabled, mythic past" of order,[57] and he comments on the way "that the anxiety over [how] such prospects should specifically play itself out in the medium of film and cyberpunk fiction warrants closer attention."[58] It is fitting that Pfau addresses how paranoia plays out in Bryan Singer's *X-Men* franchise, because I propose that forms of paranoia also play themselves out in comics. The importance in such a step is in the way we expand on the existing discourse of comics studies by shifting its concerns from trauma to paranoia as a historical experience represented in the medium. Pfau's discussion might seem to limit popular culture texts to concepts of paranoia in "late capitalism," but many different forms of paranoia emerge in Romantic literature, and these forms are both secular and religious, utilitarian and spiritual, individual and collective.

Pfau's paradigm suggests that Gaiman's, Moore and Williams's, and Carey and Gross's narrative activities intersect with Romantic narrative activities in the history of emotions: The artists use artistic spaces to express personal ways of thinking about an urgency to resist historical forces through imaginative creativity. For Pfau, such an aspect "manifests itself as a fundamental psychological climate… in a *structure of discourse*."[59] This paradigm suggests that Gaiman, Moore and Williams, and Carey and Gross become part of a larger psychological history of paranoia of which traditional literature, film, and other art forms are a part. These comic book artists *imagine* that literature is capable of achieving artistic ideals. In *Sandman*, imaginative literature sustains the integrity of human consciousness by communicating "shadow-truths" about the world;[60] in *The Unwritten*, imaginative fiction shares a "symbiotic" relationship with human integrity;[61] and in *Promethea*, imaginative creativity reconnects humankind to the divine by populating the human mind with highly idyllic characters. In this framework, imaginative creativity sets and sustains guidance for humankind's understanding of reality and how one ought to live. The larger implication for the discourse of comics studies is that these interpretations of the world and artists' place in it are part of an ongoing emotional experience that energizes creativity. With this paradigm, we can add to current conversations about Romanticism's relevance to comics studies and read the ways in which comics contain structures of a historically distinctive mood: Paranoia.

Romantic Literary Histories in Comics

Each chapter that follows shows us what happens when we argue for a more formal interpretation of historical representation in *Sandman*, *Promethea*, and *The Unwritten*. Gaiman, Moore and Williams, and Carey and Gross use the aesthetic space of comics to reinterpret literary history's relationship with humankind, and a diachronic framework suggests that *Sandman*, *Promethea*, and *The Unwritten* descend from a greater Romantic literary history. In Chapter One, I explore Gaiman's connection to Romanticism by reading how he builds the author G. K. Chesterton into "the heart" of *Sandman*'s mythology—within Morpheus's realm of The Dreaming.[62] Chesterton appears in the series as the character Fiddler's Green, and the author's place in the mythology suggests that Gaiman reflexively constructs an intimate relationship with Chesterton through the

Dream Lord. From here, I examine Chesterton's place in literary history as a descendent of Romanticism, and I comparatively read his faith in fantasy literature with the way Gaiman portrays fantasy literature in *Sandman*. I conclude that this comparative reading concretely addresses the persistence of Romantic faith from the nineteenth century, up through the early twentieth century, and into modern-day comic books with *Sandman*. Even more important, however, in this chapter I explore the ways that *Sandman* helps us reread and better understand Chesterton's place in literary history.

In Chapter Two, I trace Moore and Williams's *Promethea* to early twentieth-century occult movements that have roots in Romanticism. I first read the *Promethea* mythology as a continuation of Christian Kabbalist, or hermetic, traditions energized by Aleister Crowley and the Hermetic Order of the Golden Dawn. In the series, the mythical figure Promethea is the patron of a realm from which all imaginative creativity emanates: The Immateria. This space/place is constructed as "*the* imagination,"[63] and it becomes the highest plane of the material world in a larger metaphysical system: the Kabbalist Tree of Life. In this frame of knowledge, The Immateria becomes humankind's connection to God, or what we call "God," and artists assume responsibilities to reconnect humanity to the divine. I then trace the hermetic tradition's literary history from early twentieth-century authors, such as W. B. Yeats, to the French Symbolist movement and, finally, to Romanticism. From here, I argue that if we explore Moore and Williams's myth in relation to the hermetic worldview, it creates opportunities to better understand earlier literary projects that continue to energize comics creativity. I conclude by exploring how the endurance of the hermetic imagination in *Promethea* lends to the idea that Romanticism is part and parcel of ongoing projects of modernity to which comics are connected.

Chapter Three is the only chapter that requires a synchronic approach. In this chapter, I discuss Carey and Gross's *The Unwritten* in terms of its intersections with Romantic "organicism." This organicism is a form of Romantic faith that emerges in the narrative ways that the artists reconstruct storytelling as part of a larger organic system of stories linked to human integrity. The mythical figure Leviathan symbolizes a *living* story system, and the logic of the narrative is that human integrity bears a symbiotic relationship with the imaginative storytelling for which this figure is responsible. In the story, authors wage war against a secret society, named The Unwritten, and this war is defined by the ways these authors present the society's attempts to kill Leviathan for political power and influence. The character Lizzie Hexam comments, "I learn about how stories work for the same reason that soldiers learn how to strip a rifle."[64] Lizzie's comments capture the narrative's ideas that artists must weaponize imaginative fiction to defend and liberate humankind from tyranny and oppression. The premise of a literary war in *The Unwritten* acts as a springboard to discuss paranoia in my final chapter, because *The Unwritten*'s myth becomes less stable than *Sandman* and *Promethea*. Gaiman's and Moore and Williams's mythologies imagine fictive patterns of the ways literature provides stabilization, whereas *The Unwritten*'s mythology is one in which meaning proliferates and becomes unstable. These aesthetics suggest that the story dramatizes paranoia in the ways Carey and Gross represent artists committing to creativity that combats historical forces of tyranny and oppression.

My final chapter first examines *Sandman*, *Promethea*, and *The Unwritten* as paranoid narratives that set and sustain ideas about the urgency to create works of imaginative fiction. Then, I extend this framework to the larger discourse of the mainstream American comic book industry. I first explore how Pfau's criteria suggest that their narrative activities exhibit paranoia in the ways they portray situations of "extreme interpretive agitation and urgency."[65] In this framework, Gaiman, Moore and Williams, and Carey and Gross *imagine* the urgency for literary creativity in their myths. Pfau's ideas more importantly suggest that the narrative sense of urgency rebounds on the artists. Pfau writes, "[T]he colloquial phrase 'It takes one to know one' unwittingly throws into relief…the observer's (still contingent) affinity with the observed."[66] In other words, the narrative urgency to create art confirms the writers' own illusion of urgency to create art.

Formal aesthetics of paranoia that gathered energy in the Romantic period have persisted in comics. My final chapter demonstrates how these aesthetics extend not only to *Sandman*, *Promethea*, and *The Unwritten* but also to the larger comic book universes of which these titles are a part. Alex Romagnoli and Gian Pagnucci discuss how superhero stories often act collectively, and they can act like "evolving mythologies" that "represent culture, society, values, hopes, dreams, fears."[67] Gaiman, Moore and Williams, and Carey and Gross build mythological worlds that represent distinct values, hopes, dreams, and fears, and they extend to larger bodies of work: Thus, the comic book universe becomes partly defined by the artists' personal ideas about the relationships between creativity and human experience. The importance in reading these ideals is in the ways that it extends the discourse of comics studies and also prevailing criticism in literary studies. For instance, on one hand, Chapters One through Three observe how we can still find an embedded purposiveness to "reenchant the world"—to restore humanity's lost sense of wonder and order. In *Sandman*, *Promethea*, and *The Unwritten,* reenchantment becomes "an act of fellowship, an involvement with and concern for others rather than mere escapism."[68] The artists' creativity, in this framework, becomes a compensatory practice of sociability. On the other hand, Romantic studies suggest that authors are interpreters who are "unable and/or unwilling to recognize the condition of [their] own interpretations as constructs, fictions, and imaginary narratives."[69] In other words, the desire for "reenchantment" becomes a fiction: It is based on an artistic faith in imaginative literature. Gaiman's, Moore and Williams's, and Carey and Gross's Romantic faith is a construct, an imaginary narrative, and this faith is part of the larger discourse in the history of emotions.

Comics studies scholars tend to determine what are "appropriate" and "inappropriate" ways of engaging comics when they should remain open to insights from their own critical ancestors. This book demonstrates that we can examine a diachronic literary history of comics creativity and then trace this creativity to an earlier age of disenchantment—the Romantic Age. During this time, authors used aesthetic spaces to explore personal and collective historical experiences, and artists are still doing it. In the aesthetic space of comics, Gaiman, Moore and Williams, and Carey and Gross reimagine and reevaluate literary history and comics' relationships with it. These aesthetics typify the persistence of the Romantic state of mind, and they suggest a greater Romantic literary history of comics than prevailing scholarship leads us to believe.

Notes

1 Hillary Chute, "Comics as Literature? Reading Graphic Narrative," *PMLA*, 123, no. 2 (2008): 452, https://www.jstor.org/stable/25501865 (accessed October 18, 2021).

2 Aaron Ricker, "good reference? common mistake of ignoring the visual?" COMIXSCHOLARS-L, University of Florida LISTSERV Archives, January 15, 2019, https://lists.ufl.edu/cgi-bin/wa?A2=COMIXSCHOLARS-L;87cd81ee.1901 (accessed October 18, 2021).

3 Pascal Lefèvre, "good reference? common mistake of ignoring the visual?" COMIXSCHOLARS-L, University of Florida LISTSERV Archives, January 15, 2019, https://lists.ufl.edu/cgi-bin/wa?A2=COMIXSCHOLARS-L;77f9da8c.1901 (accessed October 18, 2021).]

4 Chute, 452.

5 Ibid., 453.

6 Ibid., 456.

7 Ibid.

8 Ibid., 459.

9 Ibid., 457.

10 Ibid.

11 Ibid., 455.

12 Ben Saunders, "Divisions in Comics Scholarship," *PMLA*, 124, no. 1 (2009): 292–93. www.jstor.org/stable/25614270 (accessed October 18, 2021).

13 Chute, 452.

14 Saunders, 292.

15 Ibid., 293.

16 Ibid., 294.

17 A period designating mainstream comics from the mid-1980s to the present.

18 I name Gaiman as the artist of *Sandman* only because he works with multiple artistic teams, whereas Carey and Gross and Moore and Williams work together for the entirety of their stories' runs.

19 Chute, 457.

20 Ibid., 459.

21 Ibid., 457.

22 See, for instance, *Promethea: Book 5*, in which Promethea visits Alan Moore and J. H. Williams III while the artists are writing and drawing *Book 5* of *Promethea*.

Alan Moore and J. H. Williams III, *Promethea: Book 5* (New York: DC Comics, 2005), 127.

23 Peter Wilkins, "An Incomplete Project: Graphic Adaptations of *Moby-Dick* and the Ethics of Response," in *Transforming Anthony Trollope: Dispossession, Victorianism and Nineteenth-Century Word and Image*, ed. Simon Grennan and Laurence Grove (Belgium: Leuven University Press, 2015), 225.

24 Cyril Camus, "Neil Gaiman: A Portrait of the Artist as a Disciple of Alan Moore," *Studies in Comics*, 2, no. 1 (2011): 148, https://doi.org/10.1386/stic.2.1.147_1 (accessed October 18, 2021).

25 Roderick McGillis, "The Sustaining Paradox: Romanticism and Alan Moore's *Promethea* Novels," in *Time of Beauty, Time of Fear: The Romantic Legacy in the Literature of Childhood*, ed. James Holt McGavran, Jr. (Iowa City: University of Iowa Press, 2012), 206, www.jstor.org/stable/j.ctt20q1tn5 (accessed October 18, 2021).

26 Throughout this book, I use Isaiah Berlin's ideas about the time frame of the Romantic period: "I do not propose to generalise [*sic*], but to convey in some other way what it is that I think romanticism to be…I think that in those years, say 1760 to 1830, something transforming occurred." This wariness of falling into the trap of providing a precise time frame works well with my later argument that Romantic ways of thinking persisted from this time period, up through the late nineteenth century, and into the twentieth and twenty-first centuries.

Isaiah Berlin, *The Roots of Romanticism* (Princeton: Princeton University Press, 1999), 1, 8.

27 Deidre Lynch and Jack Stillinger, "William Blake: 1757–1827," in *The Norton Anthology of English Literature*, ed. Stephen Greenblatt, vol. 2 (New York: W. W. Norton & Co., 2006), 77.

28 David Kunzle, "Preface," in *Rodolphe Töpffer: The Complete Comic Strips* (Jackson: University of Mississippi Press, 2007), ix.

29 Chute, 452.

30 Aaron Meskin, "Comics as Literature?" *British Journal of Aesthetics*, 49, no. 3 (2009): 224, doi:10.1093/aesthj/ayp025 (accessed October 18, 2021).

31 Ibid., 239.

32 See Richard Reynolds, *Super Heroes: A Modern Mythology* (Jackson: University Press of Mississippi, 1992); Alex Romagnoli and Gian Pagnucci, *Enter the Superheroes: American Values, Culture, and the Canon of Superhero Literature* (Lanham: Scarecrow Press, 2013), 14; George Kovacs and C. W. Marshall, *Classics and Comics* (New York: Oxford University Press, 2011).

33 See Noah Berlatsky, "Superhero Stories Aren't Myths. They're Anti-Myths," *Pacific Standard*, April 23, 2018, https://psmag.com/social-justice/superhero-stories-arent-myths-theyre-anti-myths (accessed October 18, 2021).

See also Ben Saunders, *Do the Gods Wear Capes? Spirituality, Fantasy, and Superheroes* (New York: Continuum, 2011).

See also Orion Ussner Kidder, "superheroes as myths," COMIXSCHOLARS-L, University of Florida LISTSERV Archives, April 23, 2018, https://lists.ufl.edu/cgi-bin/wa?A2=COMIXSCHOLARS-L;7dc42115.1804 (accessed October 18, 2021).

34 I have written elsewhere that "Tolkien's myth-making, Lovecraft's mythos, Tennyson's Arthurian myth-making, and the Romantics' affinities to myth-making don't quite fit the models of myth-making" that prevailing criticism thinks about in comparative studies. Nick Katsiadas, "superheroes as myths," COMIXSCHOLARS-L, University of Florida LISTSERV Archives, April 23, 2018, https://lists.ufl.edu/cgi-bin/wa?A2=COMIXSCHOLARS-L;afc5bc32.1804 (accessed October 18, 2021).

35 Kyle P. Johnson, "Sequential Narrative in the Shield of Achilles," in *Classics and Comics*, ed. George Kovacs and C. W. Marshall (New York: Oxford University Press, 2011).

36 Ekphrasis defines a creative process by which an author describes a visual work of art in detail.

37 Ibid., 54.

38 He writes, "It seems to me to be the greatest single shift in the consciousness of the West that has occurred, and all the other shifts which have occurred in the course of the nineteenth and twentieth centuries appear…in comparison less important, and at any rate deeply influenced by it."

Isaiah Berlin, *The Roots of Romanticism* (Princeton: Princeton University Press, 1999), 1–2.

39 Ibid., 2.

40 Ibid., 3.

41 Ibid., 119.

42 M. H. Abrams, *Natural Supernaturalism: Tradition and Revolution in Romantic Literature* (New York: W. W. Norton & Co., 1971), 192–93.

43 Friedrich von Schiller, *On the Aesthetic Education of Man*, in *The Norton Anthology of Theory and Criticism* (New York: W. W. Norton & Co., 2010), 491.

44 Michael Saler, *As If: Modern Enchantment and the Literary Prehistory of Virtual Reality* (New York: Oxford University Press, 2012), 19.

45 Ibid.

46 Ibid., 5.

47 Joshua Landy and Michael Saler, *The Re-Reenchantment of the World: Secular Magic in a Rational Age* (Stanford: Stanford University Press, 2009), 2.

48 Saler, 31.

49 William Buckler, *The Victorian Imagination: Essays in Aesthetic Exploration* (New York: New York University, 1980), 37.

50 M. H. Abrams, 146.

51 James Young, "The Holocaust as Vicarious Past: Art Spiegelman's *Maus* and the Afterimages of History," *Critical Inquiry*, 24, no. 3 (1998): 669–70.

52 Berlin, 49.

53 Ibid., 100.

54 Ibid., 122.

55 Ibid., 124.

56 Thomas Pfau, *Romantic Moods: Paranoia, Trauma, and Melancholy, 1790–1840* (Baltimore: Johns Hopkins University Press, 2005), 82.

57 Ibid., 83.

58 Ibid., 82.

59 Ibid., 6.

60 Neil Gaiman, *Sandman: Dream Country* (New York: DC Comics, 1990), 74.

61 Mike Carey and Peter Gross, *The Unwritten: The Wound* (New York: DC Comics, 2013), 48.

62 Neil Gaiman, *Sandman: The Doll's House* (New York: DC Comics, 1990), 197.

63 Alan Moore and J. H. Williams III, *Promethea: Book 1* (New York: DC Comics, 2000), 125.

64 Mike Carey and Peter Gross, *The Unwritten: Tommy Taylor and the Bogus Identity* (New York: DC Comics, 2010), 63.

65 Pfau, 80–81.

66 Ibid., 80.

67 Alex Romagnoli and Gian Pagnucci, *Enter the Superheroes: American Values, Culture, and the Canon of Superhero Literature* (Lanham: Scarecrow Press, 2013), 2.

68 Saler, 18.

69 Pfau, 78.

CHAPTER 1

Dreaming Kin: Neil Gaiman's *Sandman*, G. K. Chesterton, and Romantic Faith

Sandman: Transforming Literary History into Myth

Neil Gaiman's *Sandman* is a fruitful starting point to begin exploring the creative process of inventing a mythology and reimagining literary history with it. Gaiman helped energize certain creative practices in the mainstream American comic book industry, and a large body of work emerges from *Sandman*. Several *Sandman* spin-off titles make use of the series's mythology, including *Death: The High Cost of Living*, *Lucifer*, *Books of Magic*, *Dead Boy Detectives*, *The Dreaming*, *Endless Nights*, *Dream Hunters*, and many more. The mythology also provides a backdrop for the larger DC Universe.[70] In particular, *Sandman* helps us begin to understand how comic book artists build relationships with the literary past. The importance in this framework rests not only in how it can serve as a critical model to help us understand the ways in which artists establish relationships with literary history, but also how such relationships connect comics to larger, historically distinct literary projects.

In terms of narrative, *Sandman* follows the title character Morpheus, otherwise known as Dream,[71] who is part of a family of deities called The Endless. The Endless are greater than gods, and they personify what are represented as seven fundamental human experiences: Destiny, Death, Dream, Destruction, Desire, Despair, and Delirium.[72] Each deity presides over a realm beyond the "real" world from which they can influence human activities, and when it suits their purposes, they can walk among humankind. Morpheus presides over The Dreaming, a space/place that connects all human consciousness into one shared dream-world. Throughout the narrative, Gaiman highlights the relationship that the Lord of Dreams has with historically based human activities, such as the reign of the Roman Emperor Augustus Caesar, Maximilien Robespierre in the French Revolution, and Christopher Marlowe and William Shakespeare in the English Renaissance. Genre-based studies[73] suggest that historical representation in comics creates opportunities to explore an artist's personal relationship with history, and if we extend this framework to *Sandman*, it creates opportunities to explore Gaiman's personal relationships with history.

More important to Gaiman's personal relationships with history is how he highlights the history of storytelling within each of the historical periods represented in *Sandman*. Morpheus and The Dreaming are constructed as the sources from which all imaginative literature emanates. The logic follows how every story ever "dreamed" comes from Morpheus's realm, and the stories housed within The Library of Dream drive human experience. The library's caretaker, Lucien, explains that The Library of Dream holds "Every book that's ever been dreamed. Every book that's ever been imagined. Every book that's ever been lost. Millions upon millions of them."[74] Throughout *Sandman*, we as readers learn that Dream is responsible for maintaining his realm and stimulating the human imagination, and one way that he fulfills these duties is by energizing literary creativity. Authors become extensions of the power of Dream: His existence depends on dreamers and, more importantly, on dreaming authors.

If we keep in mind the importance of literary history to Dream, we can better understand the importance of literary history to Gaiman's creative process throughout the series. This reading suggests that *Sandman* challenges the generic boundaries between fiction and nonfiction that comics studies scholars tend to construct.[75] At face value, Gaiman constructs a mythology within the larger DC Universe. Within the first few issues, we see Dream interact with John Constantine, Martian Manhunter, and Scott Free (Mister Miracle). A closer examination of creative process, however, suggests that Gaiman converts literary history into a dream-based mythology, and he uses the myth as a vehicle to convey personal ideas about literature's connections to humankind's state of being. This framework suggests that Dream of The Endless is the artistic symbol and spokesperson for Gaiman's personal ideas about the power of literature to drive human history. What becomes important in terms of *Sandman*'s historical representation is that Gaiman's portrayal of literary history intersects with an author who appears alongside Morpheus in the story's mythology: G. K. Chesterton. Much scholarship on *Sandman* is wont to focus on William Shakespeare as being Gaiman's "gold standard"[76] of authorship because Gaiman recreates the Bard's career throughout three issues. However, what is less obvious and unexplored in the discourse are the ways that Gaiman elevates Chesterton above all the authors who appear in the story and how Chesterton's presence signals what or who affects Gaiman's ways of thinking about Shakespeare's career.

We first need to recollect Shakespeare's three appearances in *Sandman* to begin understanding how Chesterton affects Gaiman's ways of thinking about literary history. Shakespeare makes his debut in the issue titled "The Men of Good Fortune" (Issue 13), and Gaiman envisions him as an aspiring playwright who is found wanting tact. At an inn, Shakespeare tells Christopher Marlowe that he would "give anything to have [Marlowe's] gifts. Or more than anything to give men dreams, that would live on long after [he is] dead." The Lord of Dreams overhears these comments and interrupts: "I heard your talk, Will. Would you write great plays? Create new dreams to spur the minds of men? Is that your will?" "It is," Shakespeare replies.[77] They strike a bargain: Shakespeare will write two plays as a tribute to Dream in exchange for the power of dreams—one at the beginning and one at the end of his career. The *Sandman* issue titled "A Midsummer Night's Dream" (Issue 19) recreates Shakespeare completing the first of the two plays: *A Midsummer Night's Dream*. In this issue, Shakespeare travels with Lord Strange's Men to meet Morpheus and submit the play. After their meeting, Shakespeare and his company perform the play for the Faerie host that appears in the play itself, including Titania, Auberon, and Puck. Shakespeare's third and final appearance is in the final issue of *Sandman*'s original run (Issue 75), and it is titled "The Tempest." In this issue, Shakespeare finishes what is allegedly his final play, *The Tempest*, and submits it to Morpheus before retiring from playwriting.

An oversight in current scholarship is an exploration of how Gaiman reconstructs the historical function of Shakespeare's plays, generally, and *A Midsummer Night's Dream*, specifically. For instance, many scholars focus on whether Gaiman maintains fidelity to *A Midsummer Night's Dream* when adapting the play,[78] and these concerns tend to keep scholarship from exploring different lines of thought. In *Sandman*, for instance, Morpheus energizes Shakespeare's creativity with one specific goal—to sustain the integrity of the human psyche—and to achieve this goal, he channels *A Midsummer Night's Dream* to sustain the existence of the *fae* in the human imagination. In *Sandman*'s "A Midsummer Night's Dream," it is revealed that the *fae* are leaving the mortal world, never to return, which spurs Morpheus to maintain the realm of Faerie in the minds of the world's dreamers. During Shakespeare and company's performance, Morpheus tells Auberon, "They shall not forget you. That was important to me: that King Auberon and Queen Titania will be remembered by mortals, until this age is gone."[79] The logic is that Dream sees Faerie dreams—fairy tales—as serving an important function in human consciousness. This frame of knowledge suggests that in *Sandman*, fantasy literature fulfills some psychical, imaginative need for humankind. What matters to this historical representation of Shakespeare's *A Midsummer Night's Dream* is that it is a historical anachronism: Gaiman's ways of thinking about fantasy literature and the importance of the *fae* to the human psyche were not energized during the time of Shakespeare's England; they were energized in England during the early twentieth century, with writers such as Chesterton, J. R. R. Tolkien, and, among others, C. S. Lewis.

Fig. 2.1
The exact image that Neil Gaiman and his team of artists reproduce in *Sandman: The Doll's House*. Image courtesy of the Everett Collection.

A strong case can be made that Gaiman's ways of thinking about fantasy literature in *Sandman* were energized by Chesterton and other early twentieth-century artists—all of whom he praises as shaping him as a writer. In a 2004 speech to the Mythopoeic Society, Gaiman explains that

> Chesterton and Tolkien and Lewis were…not only the writers I read between the ages of six and thirteen, but they were the authors I read over and over again; each of them played a part in building me. Without them, I cannot imagine that I would have become a writer, and certainly not a writer of fantastic fiction. I would not have understood that the best way to show people true things is from a direction that they had not imagined the truth coming, nor that the majesty and the magic of belief and dreams could be a vital part of life and writing.[80]

Gaiman's beliefs in fantasy literature's "majesty" and its potential to become a "vital part" of one's life are found within *Sandman*'s representation of *A Midsummer Night's Dream*. Gaiman constructs Shakespeare's fairy tale as containing an artistic power vital to humankind's state of mind. What is missing from the critical conversation is that such beliefs are traceable to the work of a writer who "instructed" and "built" Gaiman to be an author of the fantastic, to an author who appears in *Sandman*—Chesterton. Shakespeare might take up more space on the pages of *Sandman*, but Gaiman enthrones Chesterton in The Dreaming, a space/place over which his symbol of artistic power (Dream) presides.

Fig. 2.2
An image of G. K. Chesterton's signature that Neil Gaiman and his team of artists reproduce in *Sandman: The Doll's House* just below the photograph. Image courtesy of the Wellesley College Library, Special Collections.

The first tell-tale sign that Chesterton is a unique figure in the *Sandman* series is that even though he is a historically based author, he is not represented as an author. Instead, Chesterton is elevated into a mythical dream-entity named Fiddler's Green. Fiddler's Green is visually represented as Chesterton, and Gaiman reinforces the connection between Chesterton and the character by reproducing a photograph of the author from the Everett Collection, accompanied by his signature (see figures 2.1 and 2.2).[81] Moreover, Gaiman constructs this entity as "the heart" of The Dreaming[82]—as the heart and center of a dream-world that symbolizes the place from which storytelling emanates. Chesterton's place at "the heart" of the mythology invites inquiries into historical representation in *Sandman*, and this structure certainly suggests that Chesterton is a more important character than what scholarship has addressed. Curious readers may discover that, like Gaiman, Chesterton is an author whose reputation is largely based on strong commitments to advocate and defend fantasy literature, and if we bear this understanding in mind when approaching *Sandman*, it suggests that the author's place in the mythology signals what or who energizes Gaiman's commitments to write fantasy fiction—to write *Sandman*. I maintain that it is no coincidence that both writers engage a particular advocacy of fantasy literature, and it is no coincidence that they both look to Shakespeare's *A Midsummer Night's Dream* as containing a creative energy that maintains humankind's unity. *Sandman*'s narrative design suggests that Gaiman represents Chesterton at the core of a mythology and deliberately connects his storytelling with Chesterton to symbolize a creative force of narrative.

We can better understand Chesterton's structural influence on Gaiman's ways of portraying literary history in *Sandman* by comparatively reading Chesterton's ideas about fantasy literature with the series's representation of fantasy literature. We must create many threads to sustain such an inquiry, but Chesterton's presence not only indicates the ways that Gaiman thinks about the historical functions of fantasy literature, but also how he thinks about his own creativity's historical function. This reading brings new insights regarding the ways that mainstream artists represent and build relationships with history, and it also brings new understandings to comics' connections to a greater literary history of Romanticism. Chesterton's presence in the mythology signals what or who affects the texture of Gaiman's historical representation, and this chapter approaches *Sandman* not only as a form of historical and personal expression but also a narrative in which Gaiman deliberately forms relationships with literary traditions. The importance of *Sandman* to this study is at least twofold: It leads us to better understandings of Gaiman's creative relationships with Chesterton, and it also sheds light on Chesterton's and Gaiman's place in a greater literary history that extends from Romanticism. A greater literary history of comics exists, and *Sandman* also helps us arrive at better understandings of literary history: Comics can help us better understand literature.

The Discourse of *Sandman*, Narrative Design, and Comics History

Chesterton's place at "the heart" of Gaiman's mythology is almost wholly overlooked in *Sandman*'s critical narrative. David Bratman describes Fiddler's Green as "a wonderful homage" to Chesterton,[83] and Ben Indick describes the character as representing "one of [Gaiman's] favorites."[84] Fiddler's Green becomes the "standard mythological motif [of the guardian]" in Stephen Rauch's comparative study of *Sandman* and Joseph Campbell's Monomyth cycle.[85] Many possible reasons exist for the critical oversight of the character's importance in the story and the author's importance to Gaiman's creativity, but in any case, we can follow Gaiman's effort to construct a relationship with Chesterton—through Chesterton's identity as a writer of fantasy literature. Gaiman deliberately builds Chesterton into the core of his mythology. His pride of place among the authors represented in *Sandman* is concrete, not speculative. The importance in exploring Chesterton's privileged place in *Sandman* is that it opens doors to better understandings of his influences on Gaiman's ways of thinking about Shakespeare and his own storytelling, while also helping us to (re-)read and better understand Chesterton and Gaiman as participants in larger creative projects that have roots in Romanticism. However, we first need to take into account Gaiman's narrative design and the creative history of this design before making the bridge from *Sandman* to Chesterton and, then, to Romanticism.

In prevailing criticism of *Sandman*, we meet one difficulty in identifying intersections between Gaiman's creative process and earlier periods of literary history: The critical narrative tends to limit his creative processes to postmodern notions of metafiction and hybridity. The distinction between these two terms is that metafiction describes narrative activities in which an artist "draw[s] attention to the artifice of storytelling" while engaged in storytelling,[86] and hybridity describes a process in which a writer pieces together a "medley of references" from prior works to create a new composition.[87] Chris Dowd, for example, extends the concept of metafiction to *Sandman* and Gaiman's larger body of work, describing his creative processes as literary dissections: "For Gaiman, metafiction is a surgical tool. He throws slabs of mythology, fairy tale, and horror onto the autopsy table and cuts into them like a mad scientist, turning them inside out to see how they are built. And then he beckons us closer to have a look at the carcass and shows us something we could have never seen otherwise."[88] In this vein, metafiction becomes an activity of narrative deconstruction. Similarly, Stephen Rauch describes *Sandman* as a "'metanarrative,' a story about stories... [that] emerges as a hybrid text, with oral and written elements, in a blending of myth and folklore. More than that, Dream is, simply put, the reason we tell stories."[89] Here, Rauch reads *Sandman* as an artistic hybrid that brackets together various storytelling traditions, and like Dowd, he suggests that Gaiman uses Morpheus to create interactions with creative sources that he imitates. These studies typify critical treatments of *Sandman* that position Gaiman using Morpheus as a vehicle for postmodern storytelling. Chesterton's place at the heart of *Sandman*, however, suggests a distinct and distinctly different mode of storytelling.

We need to open doors to new ways of rethinking the creative process and the literary history of *Sandman*. Instead of metafiction and hybridity, Cyril Camus's study of Neil Gaiman's career offers an alternative entry point by focusing the narrative practice of "integrative fiction."[90] Camus constructs a framework to read this practice in Gaiman's narrative designs, and he traces them to late 1960s and early 1970s fantasy literature. Such a critical engagement provides a foundation on which we can build better understandings of the artist's narrative connections with literary histories beyond postmodernism. It is worth noting that Camus, too, acknowledges how the "importance of intertextuality and metafiction in [their] narrative practice has often led commentators to call Gaiman and [Alan] Moore 'postmodern' comics-writers."[91] Camus sidesteps this critical consensus in a more productive vein, broadly examines the artists' narrative designs, and traces them to a common literary ancestor: Phillip José Farmer's Wold Newton stories.

In order to fully understand Gaiman's and Moore's connections to Farmer, it is necessary to examine details about *Sandman*'s publication history and place in comics history. These details help us better understand Gaiman's artistic ambitions in *Sandman* and the series's artistic legacy. When *Sandman* debuted in 1989, it appeared as a monthly serialized publication, and its original run of 75 issues was then republished as a ten-volume set of graphic novels. In addition to various *Sandman* spin-off titles written by Gaiman, such as *Death: The High Cost of Living*, *The Dream Hunters*, and (among others) *The Books of Magic*, many other spin-off titles were not written by Gaiman, such as Jill Thompson's *Little Endless Storybook* and DC Comics's *Lucifer* series.[92] In 2013, Gaiman also revisited *Sandman* with artist J. H. Williams III, and they published a six-issue prequel titled *Sandman: Overture*. The title suggests that the events in this story are structured to precede and also lead into "The Sleep of the Just," the first issue of the original series. In August 2018, Gaiman debuted *The Sandman Universe*, a one-shot comic that introduced four separate titles with four teams of artists.[93] In short, a large body of work emerges from *Sandman*, and all the artists considered in this book are connected to it.

Sandman's importance in comics history rests in how it was a flagship fantasy series that emerged within an era called "The Dark Age of Comics." This Dark Age is defined by mainstream titles published from about 1981 until 1992, and it was a remarkable time of artistic innovation in the mainstream comic book industry. Alex Romagnoli and Gian Pagnucci characterize this period as a time when many comic book artists turned narrative in on itself. Meaning, it is a time when modes of self-reflexivity and narrative deconstruction became energized, and artists used such techniques to explore, test, and experiment with characters and genres with "adult-oriented value systems."[94] Instead of the "perfect worlds"[95] that superheroes inhabited in the Golden, Silver, and Bronze ages of comics, stories like Alan Moore and Dave Gibbons's *Watchmen* debuted, where the narrative explores questions of what would happen if superheroes were introduced to the real world, which becomes disastrous and apocalyptic; and Frank Miller released *The Dark Knight Returns*, a psychological exploration of an older Bruce Wayne, who comes out of retirement to save Gotham City, during which he faces a Superman whose ideals of Truth, Justice, and the American Way are compromised by the interests of his employer, the U.S. Government. Social and political commentary as well as self-reflexive modes of creativity that rethink genre, identity, and the place of superheroes in American culture define the Dark Age, and artists turn to different value systems in comics. The emergence of these aesthetics in the medium is important to *Sandman* in the ways that Gaiman experiments with genre and explores artistic identity within a fantasy series connected to the DC Universe of which Batman, Superman, and Wonder Woman are a part. What distinguishes Gaiman's turn to "adult-oriented value systems," though, is largely based on a shift to literary value systems—as with many British artists during this Dark Age.

While Romagnoli and Pagnucci focus on the aesthetic innovations in mainstream comics during the 1980s and name this period the Dark Age, Greg Carpenter addresses this period as the

"British Invasion." Carpenter acknowledges that not "all of the innovative work was coming from British creators," but he also argues that the '80s was a time when Alan Moore, Neil Gaiman, and Grant Morrison came to America from the United Kingdom and "brought a combination of respect, audacity, and ambition necessary to transform the artistic standards of the medium."[96] With such creative ambition, these writers brought a passionate love for traditional literature to the industry, and they consciously construct narrative relationships between the popular form of comic books—a medium usually considered "lowbrow"—and "highbrow" literature. Although we should not make the mistake of reading the British Invasion in some uniform way, as Terrence Wandtke warns us,[97] what we can safely say is that Gaiman, Moore, and Morrison share a primary concern with showing the relevance of their creativity to the literary imagination.

From Gaiman, Moore, and Morrison, we see a massive influx of preexisting literary ideas, devices, and designs across the industry. Carpenter highlights how these artists acted as forerunners in a larger creative project that gave artistic legitimacy to mainstream comics in America. He likens their impact to "Marlowe, Shakespeare, and Jonson, elevating the English language into a vehicle for poetic drama. They are Coleridge, Byron, and Shelley, defining Romanticism with both their poetry and their lives."[98] These comparisons to some of the greatest writers in literary history give some heft to the artists' reputations in mainstream comics: Their contributions provided foundations on which their contemporaries and succeeding generations of mainstream comic book artists could build—and on which they are still building, nearly thirty years later. *Sandman* put Gaiman on the map as one of the most significant and influential writers in the industry, and although his love for literature energized much of his creative process, the beginnings of his successful career can be largely attributed to his mentor, Alan Moore.

The importance of Gaiman's professional relationship with Moore cannot be underestimated in better understanding his creative practices in *Sandman*. The narrative designs that Moore brought to the industry energized patterns of creativity that persist both in their work and in other titles, including *Promethea* and *The Unwritten*. Camus's contributions to the discourse are useful in at least two ways: Where Romagnoli, Pagnucci, and Carpenter broadly examine narrative practices in the industry during the '80s and early '90s, Camus focuses on the details of Moore's professional and narrative influences on Gaiman as well as their shared literary history. Camus first examines the relationship that Gaiman developed with Moore as a "contemporary influence."[99] He covers many details of their professional relationship, but he nicely condenses it in one statement: "Moore's *Swamp Thing*...rekindled [Gaiman's] interest in comics in his adulthood, and Moore was then led to personally teach him how to format a comics-script, and gave him some feedback on his first attempts."[100] For Camus, the importance of Moore's mentorship rests in having a better understanding of the ways he taught Gaiman how to write comics and also the writers' shared literary history in what is known as the Wold Newton Universe (WNU).[101]

Gaiman's *Sandman* and Moore's *Saga of the Swamp Thing* are structurally similar to Farmer's Wold Newton stories in the sense that they bring together preexisting literary characters into one shared imaginary world. In the WNU, Farmer brings together characters ranging from Edgar Rice Burroughs's Tarzan and Lester Dent's Doc Savage to Sir Arthur Conan Doyle's Sherlock Holmes and H. Rider Haggard's Allan Quatermain. To provide logic for their relationships with each other, Farmer takes the historical event of the 1795 Wold Cottage meteorite and fuses it with structures of science fiction. He then designs a "genealogical framework according to which various characters from popular literature were relatives."[102] Camus goes on to cite how Gaiman and Moore explicitly express their interests in creating their own Wold Newton worlds, and their key to bringing together preexisting literary figures rests in invented mythology.

Moore's connections to the WNU are first found in the introduction to *Book 1* of the *Saga of the Swamp Thing* series. In it, he describes his creative scope and addresses the breadth of material from which he draws:

> The continuity-expert's nightmare of a thousand different super-powered characters coexisting in the same continuum can, with the application of a sensitive and sympathetic eye, become a rich and fertile mythic background with fascinating archetypal characters hanging around, waiting to be picked like grapes on the vine...
>
> Imagine for a moment a universe jeweled with alien races ranging from the transcendentally divine to the loathsomely Lovecraftian. Imagine a cosmos where the ancient gods still exist somewhere and where whole dimensions are populated by anthropomorphic funny animals. Where Heaven and Hell are demonstrably real and even accessible, and where angels and demons alike seem to walk the earth with impunity.[103]

Here, we see Moore's ideas about creating a mythology where characters from a broad array of artistic creativity exist.[104] This creative scope matters to *Sandman* in at least two respects: On one hand, Camus addresses how Moore's work "was then, if not a direct inspiration for Gaiman's, at least the work of a *forerunner*, of which Gaiman was very much aware since *Swamp Thing* had...a tremendous impact on Gaiman's work in general, and particularly on *Sandman*."[105] Throughout *Sandman*, for example, we as readers see

Morpheus interact with characters from various cultural mythologies, including Greco-Roman, Norse, and Egyptian gods; characters from sacred texts, including the Hebrew Bible, Kabbalah, and the Bible; from the DC Universe, including The Justice League; and (among others) characters from traditional literature, including the *fae* from Shakespeare's *A Midsummer Night's Dream*. It is this creative scope where it may be logical to read how Moore's Wold Newton design for *Swamp Thing*'s mythic background became a creative model for Gaiman when he wrote *Sandman*.

On the other hand (and more importantly), Camus's research shows us what happens if we delimit the critical narrative from postmodern notions of metafiction and hybridity, and if we take Camus's study one step further, we can read how Gaiman bases his mythology on the WNU to bring together preexisting literary characters and also prior literary authors. For Camus, the WNU provided a literary blueprint that could be relocated within the comics medium to bring together preexisting characters, and going further, Gaiman could use this blueprint to build relationships with authors of the literary past. We can pursue better understandings of Gaiman's creative process in *Sandman* by moving Camus's framework beyond literary characters. If we explore Chesterton's place in the series, it creates opportunities to explore both Gaiman's motives for incorporating him within the mythology and the connections between comics and a greater literary history.

Dreaming Kin

Julie Sanders's and Helen Vendler's research can help us better understand at least three dynamics of *Sandman*: Gaiman's creative process, his motives for building Chesterton into the heart of the mythology, and the greater literary history of the series. Sanders works from Graham Allen's ideas about intertextuality, and she suggests that when artists relocate preexisting literary materials into a new medium, the "systems, codes, and traditions established by previous works of literature"[106] form a "structuring relationship"[107] with the narrative. In this framework, the presence of literary elements within a new medium indicates an artist's individual relationship with the literary past, and readers may identify variation in modes of thought between the original conception of literary materials and their reconstruction. These literary presences become opportunities to traverse the intentional fallacy and explore artistic motives for reworking the artistic past. Sanders writes, "[T]he creative import of the author cannot be as easily dismissed as Roland Barthes's or Michel Foucault's influential theories of the 'death of the author' might suggest."[108] In this vein, texts that incorporate preexisting literary materials enable readers to identify the artist's production of meaning. We cannot fully understand this production of meaning unless we cooperate and follow the artist's initiatives to reconstruct the literary past and establish personal perspectives of its systems, codes, and traditions. If we extend this scope to *Sandman*, it suggests that Gaiman produces meaning by making Chesterton's identity "original." This originality rests in the ways that Gaiman constructs Chesterton's relationship with Morpheus, and this narrative design allows us to explore the series's connections with Chesterton's work.

Where Sanders stops at examining texts and their relationships with other texts, Vendler discusses what happens when writers use aesthetic spaces not only to reimagine the artistic past but also to establish personal, intimate relationships with past artists.[109] If we extend her ideas to *Sandman*, they suggest that Gaiman reimagines Chesterton and establishes intimacy with him both as a writer and as an advocate for fantasy fiction. Vendler writes, "The contemporary artist goes to the masterpieces of the past seeking an intimate presentness of instruction, colloquy, sympathy…Yet the present-day artist must resist the temptation to slide into inert imitation."[110] These qualities of instruction, colloquy, and sympathy are not so much oriented toward imitating an artist's prior work as much as they "[send] out a ray of social imagination."[111] In this way, contemporary artists may encourage readers to understand both their range of reference to past work *and* how they use artistic spaces to identify with and receive instruction from "kindred spirit[s]."[112] The benefit of Vendler's framework is that if we extend it to *Sandman*, it expands on existing scholarship. For example, B. Keith Murphy discusses how "Gaiman respects the reader's intelligence, and he tests the limits of that intelligence."[113] I take this notion one step further by highlighting how Gaiman assumes that his range of reference with Chesterton may be the reader's own range of reference, and this step allows us to extend Vendler's perspectives on writers forming social relationships with past artists. This framework allows us to focus on Chesterton's place in *Sandman* and follow how Gaiman encourages us to understand the intimacy that he establishes with Chesterton through Morpheus.

The first key to understanding how Gaiman establishes intimacy with Chesterton is found in *The Doll's House* (Volume 2), in which the character Fiddler's Green makes his first appearance. *The Doll's House* follows the events of *Preludes & Nocturnes* (Volume 1). In *Preludes & Nocturnes*, Dream escapes a seventy-two-year imprisonment, discovers that his realm lies in ruins, and recovers items that empower him. *The Doll's House* picks up where Dream is almost finished rebuilding The Dreaming, and within "Part One," Gaiman uses two levels of narration to invite readers to follow him as he builds this imaginary world. He uses the ruinous state of Morpheus's realm to build items into the story. For example, Morpheus assigns Lucien to complete a census of the realm, and when completed, he reports, "Four of the major arcana are gone, sire. They are not to be found in The Dreaming."[114] These four entities include Brute and Glob, The Corinthian, and Fiddler's Green. On one narrative level, *The Doll's House* follows Morpheus as he retrieves these entities and completes the reconstruction of his realm, but on another level, each character plays a role in Gaiman's process of establishing relationships with the artistic past: The broader narrative impetus of *The Doll's House* is driven by Morpheus reasserting control over rogue dreams and bringing them back to The Dreaming, and at the same time, Gaiman uses characters as imaginative vehicles to assert control over narrative and establish connections with creative forebears.

For example, the two nightmare creatures, Brute and Glob, are from Jack Kirby and Joe Simon's Silver Age superhero version of Sandman, a.k.a. Hector Hall. Gaiman originally pitched a story featuring Hector Hall, but when he received his assignment to write *Sandman*, DC Comics's Editor Karen Berger[115] instructed him to create a new Sandman character. In an interview with Alex Amodo, Gaiman comments,

> When Karen asked what I wanted to do next, I had suggested a *Sandman* graphic novel, featuring the old Simon and Kirby 1970s incarnation because there were a few things that I thought were really interesting. I liked the idea of a character who lived in dreams, who had no objective existence. So, later, she said, "Well what about that Sandman idea?" I said, Okay. She said, "Great, but make it a new one"...I figured I should just reduce it to the basics, and what I got when I reduced it to the basics was Dream.[116]

What Gaiman created was an anthropomorphic dream—Dream—and after he submitted a proposal for the title, DC Comics's former Editor-in-Chief Jenette Kahn would go on to greenlight the publication of *Sandman*. Gaiman connected this character to the DC Universe of which Simon and Kirby's superhero version of Sandman was already a part. In this vein, Gaiman builds Brute and Glob into The Dreaming to pay tribute to his predecessors and take control of his assignment. In a similar way, The Corinthian functions as a narrative instrument on two levels. On one narrative level, the character is another rogue nightmare, a "flawed creation" that inspires serial killers during Dream's imprisonment.[117] Its absence from The Dreaming creates a narrative urgency for Morpheus to regain control over dreams. On another level, Bratman discusses how this character's role in leading a band of incompetent sociopaths serves as a way for Gaiman to establish the story's connections with horror writers: "By courageously goofing off with very dire material, Gaiman is in the company of a distinct category of great humorous horror writers such as John Bellairs and Joss Whedon."[118]

The final missing dream-entity, Fiddler's Green, is my principal focus, because he is regarded as "the heart" of The Dreaming. Otherwise known as "Gilbert" (after Gilbert Keith Chesterton), Fiddler's Green enters the scene as another dream gone rogue. Rauch correctly describes the character as "something between a person and a place."[119] It is a "place" in the sense that it appears in The Dreaming as a fertile, lush-green dreamscape, which maintains its connection to maritime folklore, and it is a "person" in the sense that during Morpheus's 72-year absence from his realm, it leaves The Dreaming in the form of a man: Chesterton. Fiddler's Green is, most importantly, "the heart" of a space/place connected to Gaiman's creativity in the ways that all imaginative creativity is an extension of Morpheus's power, and when Morpheus catches up with him, he requires the entity to take up his position once again. The Dream Lord tells Fiddler's Green, "I cannot find it in my heart to punish you for leaving. Not now. However, it is time to take up your appointed position."[120] The importance of this moment rests in the ways Gaiman identifies his creativity with the powers of the title character, Morpheus, and builds Chesterton into the core of his mythology. It establishes what Vendler calls an "intimate presentness"[121] with past artists, and Gaiman maintains Chesterton's presence in The Dreaming throughout the series. Gaiman builds Chesterton into "the heart" of the mythology near the beginning of the series, and he stays there until just before Morpheus's death in *The Kindly Ones* (Volume 9).

Gaiman builds Chesterton into a world where stories are born, and this world, ironically, symbolizes a space/place from which *Sandman* is born. In *Sandman*, every story ever dreamed comes from The Dreaming, and dreams are commensurate with stories. In this way, Gaiman maintains a personal relationship with the story's mythical figure in "creating a dream"—creating a story—and at the same time, he maintains a personal relationship with the heart of the mythology: Chesterton. Gérard Genette, from whom Sanders draws to construct her theory of adaptation, describes such a narrative design as a "movement of proximation,"[122] and Vendler's ideas about writers establishing relationships with past artists suggests that Gaiman keeps Chesterton within proximity to Morpheus to embrace him as a kindred spirit of storytelling and as an energizing force of his own creativity. Morpheus even comments that Fiddler's Green is "vavasour of his own dominion" in The Dreaming.[123] As Morpheus is Lord of the Dreaming, Fiddler's Green is a lord of his own space, and they become "dreaming kin." If we follow Gaiman's creative process of building Chesterton into The Dreaming, then we open doors to better understandings of Gaiman's imagined intimacy with him and *Sandman*'s connections to greater imaginative traditions of which Chesterton was a part. This intimacy suggests that Chesterton plays an energizing force of Gaiman's narrative practice and artistic identity in *Sandman*, and a broader literary-historical scope suggests that the series becomes an extension of larger creative projects of the early twentieth century that descended from Romanticism. What happens to Chesterton's identity as a Catholic author becomes a concern of ethical import, but his identity is not incompatible with Romantic literary history.

Ethics of Historical Representation: A Catholic Author in a Secular Narrative

The ethics of representing Chesterton in *Sandman* concern the process of absorbing a Catholic writer into a secular mythology. Within Sanders's framework, contemporary artists may "authenticate" and "revere" their references to "'authoritative,' culturally validated, texts [...or adopt] a posture of critique, even assault."[124] Artists may embrace or attack their literary forbears when representing them in new texts, and Chesterton's place in *Sandman* suggests that Gaiman embraces his creativity's relationship with Chesterton but, in the process, secularizes the author. Bratman explains Chesterton's presence in the story: "At the end of [*The Doll's House*] we find out who, or what, he really is; but I would say that the fact that something is obviously amiss here from the beginning is enough to obviate any criticism that this wonderful homage is a misappropriation in a non-Christian story."[125] Chesterton's presence in the *Sandman* mythology is more than a mere homage. A closer examination of Chesterton's creative practice and ways of thinking about fantasy literature helps us better understand not only *how* but, more importantly, *why* Gaiman incorporates the author into the *Sandman* mythology. Gaiman's social motives for establishing a relationship with Chesterton attach *Sandman* to the larger literary project of "reenchanting the world."

Alison Milbank helps us begin to understand aspects of Chesterton with which Gaiman connects in *Sandman*. She discusses Chesterton's perspectives about fantasy literature from the vantage point of his Catholic faith and the larger literary project to reenchant the modern world. She explains that part of Chesterton's artistic identity is based on theological ambitions in a mode of "Catholic and realist praxis and ethics."[126] This theological framework suggests that Chesterton's literary creativity becomes two things: a "riposte" to modern ideas of disenchantment[127] and a virtuous form of gift-giving or charity. First, Milbank characterizes how Chesterton's ideas about fantasy literature directly challenge Max Weber's famous declaration, from 1917, that we live in a "disenchanted world"—or a world bereft of magic and wonder by an increasingly secular, reason-based culture. This reading is based on Chesterton's understanding of fantasy as a mode of writing capable of "mak[ing] more luminous the simple realities of our own world,"[128] and she continues to describe how many early twentieth-century fantasy writers, including Tolkien and Lewis, "quite rightly refut[ed]" the idea that the world is disenchanted.[129] Such writers sought to create an "intellectually engaged"[130] form of reenchantment to restore humankind's sense of wonder. They understood that fantasy literature could achieve this goal by encouraging readers to understand the connections between the stories and the real world, and these ideas suggest that as Chesterton, Tolkien, and Lewis "built" Gaiman as a fantasy writer, their ideas about the redeeming qualities of fantasy literature found their way into his work on *Sandman*.

For Chesterton, the intellectually engaging aspect of fantasy functions through the literary trope of magic, and we find similar aesthetics in Gaiman's trope of dreams in *Sandman*. Chesterton suggests that the trope of magic plays a regenerative role in the health of the human mind because it bears the capabilities to remind readers of the magic that one could perceive in the world and in everyday things. In "Ethics of Elfland," for example, Chesterton explains his ideas about wonder and beauty, and he writes of magic and its relationship with the real world:

> These subconscious convictions are best hit off by the colour and tone of certain tales. Thus I have said that stories of magic alone can express my sense that life is not only a pleasure but an eccentric privilege...[131]
>
> [This] world does not explain itself. It may be a miracle with a supernatural explanation; it may be a conjuring trick, with a natural explanation. But the explanation of the conjuring trick, if it is to satisfy me, will have to be better than the natural explanations I have heard. The thing is magic, true or false.[132]

Here, Chesterton explains that the magic in fantasy literature is not irreconcilable with empirical science, and he suggests that fantasy offers people better explanations than secular reason. It offers humankind "the test of the imagination"[133] and the belief in the "remote possibility of a miracle."[134] For Chesterton, magic is all around us in the natural world, and fantasy literature helps us remember that it is there: "All that we call common sense and rationality and practicality and positivism only means that for certain dead levels of our life we forget that we have forgotten. All that we call spirit and art and ecstacy [*sic*] only means that for one awful instant we remember that we forget."[135]

Milbank continues to discuss how Chesterton's ideas about magic found their way into later fantasy writers' work, particularly

Tolkien's Middle-earth, and her ideas are useful for reading how Chesterton's beliefs in the power of fantasy literature persist in Gaiman's work. She writes, "There is…a more potent and universal magic in Tolkien's world by which the whole material cosmos is infused with a kind of enchantment, as if it had a radiance: a 'lumen'…[Magic] is a property of everything in the novel: wood, stone and iron as in the traditional fairy-tale (which of course need have no actual fairy to guarantee its 'fairy' status)."[136] In Middle-earth, readers are encouraged to understand the connection between the imaginary (magic) and the real (the material world), and this framework suggests that Tolkien seeks to "find new ways to restore language as a signifying medium of the real world: namely, by the fantastic."[137] The logic is that Tolkien's creative process is energized by a sense of responsibility to write an intellectually engaging fantasy capable of restoring humankind's sense of wonder, and the trope of magic becomes a way that fantasy writers translate the wonders of the natural world into fiction. The *Sandman* series indicates an inheritance of this literary model with its ideas that human history is undergirded by the power of dreams. "Magic" in Chesterton and Tolkien becomes Dream's powers in *Sandman*.

The second point in Chesterton's artistic model—connected with the first—is that literary creativity becomes a commitment to an ideal of artistic creation, and *Sandman* connects to this sense of artistic responsibility by constructing authors as extensions of the powers of Dream. For Chesterton and Gaiman, authorship becomes a virtuous activity energized by ideas of sacrifice, gift-giving, and charity.[138] The difference rests in the ways Chesterton's model constructs artists as becoming mediating gift-givers between humankind and the Judeo-Christian God by committing to the idea of restoring a sense of the world's wonder. Milbank writes, "In Chesterton's view, everything is waving madly at us to indicate its divine origin and its storied character. Mediation [or authorship] is therefore not a distantiation from God but an enabling of this realization of divine purpose."[139] Chesterton's ideas about literary creativity, in other words, are based on his Catholic faith in a process where artists invite readers into a method of gift-giving whose origins are divine: By imparting stories to humankind, the artist assumes responsibilities to channel the divine. In this sense, stories are undergirded or enchanted by the idea of their origin in God. We must always bear in mind that Chesterton, Tolkien, and (among others) Lewis energized and developed many ideas about the fantasy author's redeeming creativity, and Gaiman explicitly addresses the ways these writers "built" him as a fantasy writer. The *Sandman* series secularizes this literary model with its ideas that the history of storytelling is an extension of Dream, who sustains the integrity of human consciousness. Gaiman's artistic model is based on a secular faith in the redeeming qualities of fantasy literature.

Gaiman's faith in imaginative literature differs from Chesterton's faith in the ways that *Sandman*'s ideas about storytelling are undergirded by secular ideals of dreams. This intersection, however, helps us better understand where the secular and the sacred meet in this faith in imaginative literature and where in literary history we see secular and sacred forms of this faith become energized: Romanticism. The importance in this line of inquiry is that we can trace both perspectives through literary history to larger creative projects of early twentieth-century Modernism that descended from Romanticism and helped shape Chesterton's ideas about fantasy literature. This approach suggests that *Sandman* helps us reread and better understand Chesterton's place in early twentieth-century literary practices. We better understand Chesterton's place in literary history if we cooperate and follow Gaiman's initiatives to construct a relationship with Chesterton. Gaiman inherits ways of thinking about fantasy literature by way of Chesterton, and Chesterton's Catholic ideas about the virtues of storytelling emerge from Victorian and Romantic ideas about artists fulfilling moral obligations to drive human history through imaginative creativity.

Re-Reading Chesterton

Gaiman's *Sandman* helps us reread and expand on prevailing criticism about Chesterton by offering a narrative that invites us to explore the author's place and identity in The Dreaming. Exploring Gaiman's artistic motives for building Chesterton into the *Sandman* mythology leads us to better understandings of Chesterton's function within Victorian and Modernist literary projects, and such projects become a continuum of Romantic ways of thinking about imaginative creativity. Michael Ingleby's research is useful in beginning to understand Chesterton in these contexts when he explains that Chesterton is "someone with much to offer areas quite removed from religious matters as conventionally articulated. Once we separate Chesterton's observations on a range of phenomena from the question of his [Catholic] faith, he becomes at once a more amenable and more challenging figure within critical discourse."[140] We can take Ingleby's ideas about separating Chesterton from his Catholic faith a step further to help us see Chesterton's creativity in larger contexts, particularly in the larger scope of Victorian and Modernist literary projects where we see attempts to revive Romanticism's faith in imaginative creativity. William Buckler characterizes these attempts as

> literary experiment[s] which the Victorians undertook with the urgency of a desperate hope [for] the salvation of imaginative

> letters...The sense of hieratic intensity was already there: a sacred pungency had been created by Blake, Wordsworth, Keats, and Shelley and by the flow from Germany that was released into England by Coleridge and, in a more strictly literary fashion, by Carlyle...[141]
>
> It is a poetic faith that, allowing for the secularization and deflation of language, persists right through Yeats, Eliot, Stevens, and Lowell as the archetypal Romantic faith.[142]

The keys, here, are the ideas of salvaging humankind's faith in imaginative creativity and how many authors continue to commit to this larger Romantic project not only in the Victorian period but also up through the Modernist period. This poetic faith is defined by ideas about literature's capabilities to restore humanity's relationship with the sacred and to unite a fractured and fragmented world with artistic creativity. Art becomes a secular religion of modernity to the Romantics, and Buckler demonstrates how many Victorian and Modernist writers bear an "aesthetic imperative"[143] to be "both innovative and relevant" to what the "Romantics had done so conscientiously and so well."[144] We see this faith both in Chesterton and, by extension, Gaiman, but a problem we meet with reading this diachronic literary history is how much scholarship tends to separate Chesterton and other early twentieth-century fantasy writers from "high Modernism" and the Modernist endeavor to salvage imaginative literature in the popular imagination.

When combined with comics studies' approaches to historical representation,[145] Buckler's ideas that the early Modernists sought to "redefine miracles" within "new functional modes"[146] may be extended to Chesterton, Tolkien, Lewis, and their literary descendants as much as these ideas may be extended to poets such as T. S. Eliot, Ezra Pound, and W. B. Yeats. Michael Shallcross creates opportunities to extend Buckler's ideas from Chesterton to Gaiman by explaining how Chesterton functions within and outside Modernism. Shallcross's study is concerned with challenging prevailing ideas about Chesterton's identity in literary history. Such criticism imagines him "blundering his way around a hyper-refined aesthetic realm,"[147] and Shallcross seeks to recuperate Chesterton's identity by examining the author's parodic exchanges with T. S. Eliot, Katherine Mansfield, and James Joyce. He concludes that Chesterton's work is not as aesthetically intolerant and irreconcilable with high Modernism as we are led to believe,[148] and I expand on these ideas about Chesterton's participation in Modernism by considering his ways of thinking about fantasy literature's historical function. In this vein, we can think about Chesterton in terms of the persistence of Romantic faith in early twentieth-century Modernism.

Literature is a place in early twentieth-century Modernism where secular and sacred beliefs often meet, and Chesterton's and Gaiman's faith in fantasy literature's redemptive roles in human history is reconciled with Romanticism's faith in the role of art. Buckler identifies how late nineteenth- and early twentieth-century poetic modes provided "new foundations" for Romanticism's "old" beliefs in the role of art in history to develop human integrity,[149] and we find these beliefs in the ways that Chesterton and Gaiman think about fantasy literature in their work. In "The Ethics of Elfland," for example, Chesterton writes,

> I am concerned with a certain way of looking at life, which was created in me by fairy tales, but has since been meekly ratified by the mere facts…[150]
>
> [F]airy tales founded in me two convictions; first, that this world is a wild and startling place, which might have been quite different, but which is quite delightful; second, that before this wildness and delight one may well be modest and submit to the queerest limitations of so queer a kindness. But I found the whole modern world running like a high tide against both my tendernesses.[151]

Here, Chesterton explains what fantasy literature did for him when many post-Darwinian, post-Freudian sciences began to have a strong influence in Western culture. For Chesterton, Western culture's turn to secular reason had unhealthy consequences on humankind's perspectives of the natural world: "I found the whole modern world talking scientific fatalism…In fact, according to them, nothing ever really happened since the beginning of the world. Nothing ever had happened since existence had happened; and even about the date of that they were not very sure."[152] The subtext is that such modern sciences espouse ways of thinking about the world that are unhealthy for the human mind, but Chesterton refers to the "many noble and healthy principles" that "come from being fed on fairy tales."[153]

Chesterton's work foregrounds fantasy as a mode of writing capable of maintaining humankind's awareness of the active and vibrant wonders of the world, and the project to reenchant the world energized the elevation of fantasy in the public imagination. In this way, fantasy writers became allies with the Modernists in salvaging humankind's faith in imaginative literature. What matters for our purposes is that we must bear in mind that *Sandman* brings us to this understanding: Gaiman invites readers to follow and understand his artistic motives for representing Chesterton within the story, and curious readers who explore Gaiman's range of reference may be led to better understandings of Chesterton's identity in literary history. Gaiman uses the character Fiddler's Green to identify with a Chestertonian faith in fantasy literature, and although it is a secular faith, it is still defined by ideas about a writer's capabilities to gift dreams—to gift wonder—to the world through imaginative creativity. For Chesterton, fantasy literature is an aesthetic space where the real and imaginary can meet. An artist can use the tropes of magic and mythical creatures as literary devices to ascribe meaning to the world and reintroduce readers to it "as if it were seen for the first time."[154] Milbank explains that Chesterton's ideas about magic characterize a process in which the fantasy writer "makes strange" the real world and changes "the shape of the universe" as it passes through readers' minds.[155] This is a process of transforming "real things" into fiction,[156] and we find this creative process in Gaiman's mythology—in his transformation of literary history into myth, into the power of d/Dream.

Chesterton sees fantasy authors as responsible for using the language and image of magic to "reenchant" the world, and Chesterton—as a writer—assumes these responsibilities as well. He functions within his own model of artistic creativity, and Gaiman follows suit by using the language and image of d/Dream to enchant the creative process of storytelling. In *Sandman*, the figure of Dream, as well as the ways dreams are commensurate with stories, establish Gaiman's relationship with his own artistic model. Magic becomes the "property of everything" in Chesterton's and Tolkien's worlds just as Morpheus's power of dreams becomes the property of all storytelling in Gaiman's world, including his own. When readers pick up *Sandman*, they are "picking up a dream," and throughout *Sandman*, Gaiman draws readers' attention to this idea: "You must never forget that this is a dream."[157] Gaiman "makes strange" and enchants literary history with the idea of the transformational powers of dreams and storytelling. Milbank explains how many Modernist writers use a "mythic method" to construct frames of reference with the artistic past: "Modernist writing reaches back to assert the influence of earlier culture on the present through the 'mythic method,' while simultaneously stressing the gap between modernity and the past through ironic juxtaposition."[158] We find a mythic method carried out in *Sandman* in the ways that Gaiman establishes Morpheus's relationship with past authors. Gaiman juxtaposes past and present between Morpheus and Chesterton, and the intersections between the writers' ways of thinking about fantasy literature culminate in Gaiman's method of reimagining Shakespeare's *A Midsummer Night's Dream* within the *Sandman* mythology.

A Chestertonian Shakespeare in *Sandman*

Chesterton's place in *Sandman* challenges the critical consensus that out of the authors present in *Sandman*, Gaiman uses only Shakespeare as a device to develop the narrative. Joan Gordon, for example, examines how Gaiman "uses Shakespeare as a vehicle for his own experience of writing."[159] Annalisa Castaldo argues that Gaiman "creates Shakespeare as the human mirror of Dream, suffering loss and bowed under responsibility as Dream is."[160] Julia Round reads how *Sandman*'s "A Midsummer Night's Dream" exploits the darker aspects of Shakespeare's play, and she determines that *Sandman's* larger narrative has a "basis in the play's text and performance legacy."[161] Julie Myers Saxton similarly engages a comparative reading of *A Midsummer Night's Dream* and *Sandman*, and she identifies their larger intersections between theme, character, and space/place: "Although [Gaiman's 'A Midsummer Night's Dream'] makes the most transparent references to Shakespeare's play, elements of *A Midsummer Night's Dream* can be seen throughout the series, and not just for backdrop or mythological context."[162] In my prior work, I have examined how Gaiman constructs a relationship between his process of writing the final issue of *Sandman*, titled "The Tempest," and Shakespeare writing his supposed final play, *The Tempest*.[163] One overlooked aspect, however, is how Gaiman thinks about Shakespeare and reimagines the historical function of his plays.

Gaiman reinterprets Shakespeare as wielding the dream-power of fairy tales, and he mythologizes Shakespeare's *A Midsummer Night's Dream* as enchanted or energized by d/Dream. The logic of the narrative elevates fairy tales as a creative force that fulfills some psychical, imaginative need of humankind, and this way of thinking was energized by Chesterton and other early twentieth-century fantasy writers. What is more, Gaiman's ways of thinking about *A Midsummer Night's Dream* correspond with what Chesterton has said about the play. Scholarship has touched on the ways that Gaiman explores the relationships between literature and human history in *Sandman*,[164] but what is less clear is how Chesterton signals what or who affects the ways Gaiman constructs the historical function of literature. If we read Gaiman's "A Midsummer Night's Dream" alongside Chesterton's ideas about the play, it makes their connection much more concrete. For example, in his comments about the play, Chesterton writes, "*A Midsummer Night's Dream* is a psychological study, not of a solitary man, but of a spirit that unites mankind… The sentiment of such a play, so far as it can be summed up at all, can be summed up in one sentence. It is the mysticism of happiness."[165] These comments capture Chesterton's faith in fairy tales' capabilities to unite humankind by containing "an atmosphere as magic" elicits pleasure. For Chesterton, *A Midsummer Night's Dream* takes us beyond the "logical and destructive modern school"[166] and renews our perspectives on life.

By comparison, in *Sandman*'s "A Midsummer Night's Dream," we as readers learn that Dream channeled the play through

Shakespeare with the goal of sustaining the memory of the *fae* in the human imagination. It is also a psychological study of fairy tales, and in the story, it becomes an extension of Dream's duties to maintain the integrity of the human mind. While Shakespeare and his troupe perform the play, Morpheus tells Auberon and Titania, "During your stay on this Earth the faerie have afforded me much diversion, and entertainment. Now you have left, for your own haunts. And I would repay you all for the amusement and more: They shall not forget you. That was important to me: that King Auberon and Queen Titania will be remembered by mortals, until this age is gone."[167] Here, Morpheus emphasizes the importance of sustaining the *fae* in human memory, and this emphasis functions in at least two narrative ways. First, Gaiman represents Shakespeare as empowered and guided by Dream to preserve the memory of the Faerie host. The logic follows that a universal artistic power is connected to the image of the *fae*, the importance of which is sustained only in dreams and books—in *A Midsummer Night's Dream*. For Dream, "the faeries have afforded [him] much diversion and entertainment," and for humankind, the logic of the narrative constructs *A Midsummer Night's Dream* as containing the gift of "shadow-truths that will endure when mere facts are dust and ashes, and forgot."[168] These "shadow-truths" go beyond secular reason, and this belief in the truths and knowledge that fairy tales contain is an inherited artistic model that we can trace from Gaiman to Chesterton's ideas about fantasy literature, generally, and Shakespeare's *A Midsummer Night's Dream*, specifically.

Second, Gaiman is a productively self-aware artist, and this mode of narration suggests that he theorizes Faerie's importance in the minds of the world's dreamers while he is writing a fantasy filled with artistic images of the *fae*, gods and goddesses, and many other creatures from myth, fairy tales, and folklore. This mode of narration connects his story to an imaginative tradition based on faith in the power of fantasy—in the power to populate the human mind with forms of beauty that restore wonder and reenchant humankind. This faith in fantasy literature emerges with Chesterton and other fantasy writers of the early twentieth century, and the place of Fiddler's Green at the heart of The Dreaming suggests that this value system energizes Gaiman's creativity. Gaiman identifies his creativity with Dream, and he uses the figure of Dream to construct an imagined relationship with Chesterton. My point is that current scholarship is right to read how Gaiman connects his creativity in *Sandman* with Shakespeare, but only inasmuch as Gaiman's ideals of Shakespeare's authorship were energized by Chesterton and other early twentieth-century fantasy writers. The *Sandman* series does not contain a Renaissance Shakespeare; it contains a Chestertonian Shakespeare.

This chapter demonstrates that if we remain open to a greater literary history of comics, we achieve better understandings of literary history and Romanticism's lasting effects. Exploring Gaiman's motives for building Chesterton into the *Sandman* mythology also helps us better understand that comics' literary history is not limited to postmodern narrative practices. We have much more to consider when exploring historical representation and literary-historical designs in comics. A key to unlocking Gaiman's greater literary history in *Sandman* rests in examining Gaiman's range of reference and Chesterton's place at the core of the mythology. Within this framework, Gaiman's narrative practice is not limited to postmodern notions of metafiction and hybridity as prevailing scholarship leads us to believe. He uses Morpheus as a vehicle to establish intimacy with Chesterton and connect with his ideals of authorship. These ideals are defined by the potential of fantasy literature to restore meaning to human life and renew humankind's sense of wonder. The mythology of *Sandman*, then, intends to create an aesthetic experience that facilitates readers' return to better ways of perceiving the world and seeing meaning within it.

Gaiman transforms literary history with the *Sandman* mythology and establishes his creativity's relationship with a faith in imaginative literature traceable to Chesterton. These dynamics of historical representation also lead to better understandings of how Chesterton's and Gaiman's faith in fantasy literature is connected to larger literary projects of the early twentieth century that descend from Romanticism. We must remember that *Sandman* and genre-based methodologies in comics studies got us here. Other artists transform literary history with myths in comics, and comic book artists connect their creativity to other forms of Romantic faith in imaginative literature. These different forms of Romantic faith can be similar in that they are based on the belief that artists have a role in driving human history. Yet differences in Romantic faith are inevitable outcomes from the fact that myths do not remain static and fixed, nor can artists' perspectives of the imagination and creativity be stereotyped into any one particular artistic model or symbolic system. In *Sandman*, *Promethea*, and *The Unwritten*, the artists construct myths in which a persona of imagination—Morpheus, Promethea, and Leviathan—plays out a certain action and function. In the following chapters, I use this premise as a springboard to explore diverse forms of Romantic faith in comics.

Notes

70 Please see the Conclusion of this book for a longer discussion of *Sandman* and the DC Universe.

71 In the series, Morpheus is also known as Dream Lord, the Lord of Dreams, Kai'ckul, Lord L'Zoril, and other names.

72 Delirium was once called "Delight."

73 Hillary Chute, "Comics as Literature? Reading Graphic Narrative," *PMLA*, 123, no. 2 (2008): 452, https://www.jstor.org/stable/25501865 (accessed October 18, 2021).

74 Neil Gaiman, *Sandman: The Kindly Ones* (New York: DC Comics, 2012), 23.

75 For instance, see the Introduction of this book, where I explain that *Sandman* is a title that can be better understood as occupying a space between mainstream fiction and nonfiction and that the "key to this understanding rests in remaining open to insights from literary criticism."

76 Annalisa Castaldo, "'No More Yielding Than a Dream': The Construction of Shakespeare in *The Sandman*," *College Literature: A Journal of Critical Literary Studies*, 31, no. 4 (2004): 95, doi:10.1353/lit.2004.0052 (accessed October 19, 2021).

77 Neil Gaiman, *Sandman: The Doll's House* (New York: DC Comics, 1990), 114.

78 Julia Round, "Subverting Shakespeare? *The Sandman* 19: 'A Midsummer Night's Dream,'" in *Sub/Versions: Cultural Status, Genre and Critique*, ed. Pauline MacPherson, Christopher Murray, Gordon Spark, and Kevin Corstorphine (Newcastle: Cambridge Scholars Publishing, 2008); Julie Myers Saxton, "Dreams and Fairy Tales: Themes of Rationality and Love in *A Midsummer Night's Dream* and *The Sandman*," in *The Neil Gaiman Reader*, ed. Darrell Schweitzer (Holicong, PA: Wildside Press, 2007).

79 Neil Gaiman, *Sandman: Dream Country* (New York: DC Comics, 1990), 74.

80 Neil Gaiman, "A Speech I Gave Once: On Lewis, Tolkien and Chesterton," Harper Collins Publishers, January 26, 2012, http://journal.neilgaiman.com/2012/01/speech-i-once-gave-on-lewis-tolkien-and.html (accessed October 19, 2021).

81 Gaiman, *Sandman: The Doll's House*, 208.

82 Ibid., 197.

83 David Bratman, "A Game of You—Yes, *You*," in *The Sandman Papers: An Exploration of the Sandman Mythology*, ed. Joseph L. Sanders (Seattle: Fantagraphics Books, 2006), 43.

84 Ben Indick, "Neil Gaiman in Words and Pictures," in *The Neil Gaiman Reader*, ed. Darrell Schweitzer (Cabin John, PA: Wildside Press, 2007), 81.

85 Stephen Rauch, *Neil Gaiman's* The Sandman *and Joseph Campbell: In Search of Modern Myth* (Holicong, PA: Wildside Press, 2003), 55.

86 Chris Dowd, "An Autopsy of Storytelling: Metafiction and Neil Gaiman," in *The Neil Gaiman Reader*, ed. Darrell Schweitzer (Cabin John, PA: Wildside Press, 2007), 104.

87 Julie Sanders, *Adaptation and Appropriation* (New York: Routledge, 2006), 5.

88 Dowd, 104.

89 Rauch, 118.

90 Cyril Camus, "Neil Gaiman: A Portrait of the Artist as a Disciple of Alan Moore," *Studies in Comics*, 2, no. 1 (2011): 148, doi:10.1386/stic.2.1.147_1 (accessed October 19, 2021).

91 Ibid., 150.

92 Mike Carey took the helm of Vertigo's *Lucifer* series in its June 2000 debut, and Peter Gross joined the creative team in Issue 5. They were to stay on the title until August 2006.

93 Nalo Hopkinson wrote *The House of Whispers*; Kat Howard wrote *The Books of Magic*; Simon Spurrier wrote *The Dreaming*; and Dan Watters wrote *Lucifer*. In 2019, DC Comics introduced a fifth title with *Hellblazer* No. 1, with Simon Spurrier as the writer.

94 Alex Romagnoli and Gian Pagnucci, *Enter the Superheroes: American Values, Culture, and the Canon of Superhero Literature* (Lanham: Scarecrow Press, 2013), 119.

95 Ibid., 120.

96 Greg Carpenter, *The British Invasion! Alan Moore, Neil Gaiman, Grant Morrison, and the Invention of the Modern Comic Book Writer* (Edwardsville, IL: Sequart Organization, 2016), 7.

97 Terrence Wandtke, *The Comics Scare Returns: The Contemporary Resurgence of Horror Comics* (Rochester, NY: RIT Press, 2018), 127.

98 Carpenter, 9.

99 Camus, 148.

100 Ibid.

101 Ibid.

102 Ibid., 150.

103 Alan Moore, quoted in Cyril Camus, "Neil Gaiman: A Portrait of the Artist as a Disciple of Alan Moore," 149–50.

104 To reveal Gaiman's interests in integrative fiction, Camus cites the introduction to "A Study in Emerald," a short story that brings together Doyle's Sherlock Holmes and H. P. Lovecraft's Cthulhu mythos:

> As a boy I had loved Philip Jose [*sic*] Farmer's Wold Newton stories, in which dozens of characters from fiction were incorporated into one coherent world, and I had greatly enjoyed watching my friends Kim Newman and Alan Moore build their own Wold Newton-descended worlds…It looked like fun. I wondered if I could try something like that (quoted in Camus, "Neil Gaiman: A Portrait of the Artist as a Disciple of Alan Moore," 150).

From here, Camus extends Gaiman's ambition to create a Wold Newton-descended world to *Sandman* and also to Gaiman's larger body of work, both in and out of comics (Camus, "Neil Gaiman: A Portrait of the Artist as a Disciple of Alan Moore," 151).

105 Ibid., 150.

106 Sanders, 3.

107 Ibid., 5.

108 Ibid., 3.

109 Helen Vendler, *Invisible Listeners: Lyric Intimacy in Herbert, Whitman, and Ashbery* (Princeton: Princeton University Press, 2005), 57.

110 Ibid., 66.

111 Ibid., 63.

112 Ibid., 67.

113 B. Keith Murphy, "The Origins of *Sandman*," in *The Sandman Papers: An Exploration of the Sandman Mythology,* ed. Joseph L. Sanders (Seattle, WA: Fantagraphics, 2006), 18.

114 Gaiman, *Sandman: The Doll's House*, 38.

115 It must be said that Karen Berger can be largely credited with the Vertigo line of DC Comics, DC's former "mature" imprint. Titles such as Alan Moore's *Saga of the Swamp Thing*, Gaiman's *Sandman*, and Jamie DeLano's *Hellblazer* led to its creation. As editor, Berger recruited many British artists during the 1980s and early 1990s, including Moore, Gaiman, and Grant Morrison. Carpenter writes that Berger became "one of the key players in the British Invasion."

Greg Carpenter, *The British Invasion! Alan Moore, Neil Gaiman, Grant Morrison, and the Invention of the Modern Comic Book Writer* (Edwardsville, IL: Sequart Organization, 2016), 51.

116 Neil Gaiman, quoted in B. Keith Murphy, "The Origin of the Sandman," in *The Sandman Papers: An Exploration of the Sandman Mythology,* ed. Joseph L. Sanders (Seattle, WA: Fantagraphics, 2006), 15.

117 Gaiman, *Sandman: The Doll's House*, 161.

118 Bratman, "A Game of You—Yes, *You*," in *The Sandman Papers*, 44.

119 Rauch, 33.

120 Gaiman, *Sandman: The Doll's House*, 199.

121 Vendler, 66.

122 Gérard Genette, quoted in Julie Sanders, 20.

123 Gaiman, *Sandman: The Doll's House*, 40.

124 Sanders, 4.

125 Bratman, 43.

126 Alison Milbank, *Chesterton and Tolkien as Theologians: The Fantasy of the Real* (New York: T&T Clark, 2009), xv.

127 Ibid., xiv.

128 Ibid., xiii.

129 Ibid., 8.

130 Ibid., 9.

131 G. K. Chesterton, "Ethics of Elfland," in *Orthodoxy* (New York: John Lane Company, 1908), 115, https://archive.org/details/orthodoxy1909ches (accessed October 19, 2021).

132 Ibid., 117.

133 Ibid., 90.

134 Ibid., 93.

135 Ibid., 97.

136 Milbank, 42–43.

137 Ibid., 29.

138 I have written elsewhere, "*Sandman* constructs artists as heroic in sacrificing the domestic, committing to an ideal of humankind's aesthetic and, thus, moral education." Nick Katsiadas, "Mytho-Auto-Bio: Neil Gaiman's *Sandman*, the Romantics, and Shakespeare's *The Tempest*," *Studies in Comics*, 6, no. 1 (2015): 66–67, doi:10.1386/stic.6.1.61_1 (accessed October 19, 2021).

139 Milbank, 11.

140 Michael Ingleby, introduction to *G. K. Chesterton, London, and Modernity*, ed. Matthew Beaumont and Michael Ingleby (New York: Bloomsbury, 2013), 7–8.

141 William Buckler, *The Victorian Imagination: Essays in Aesthetic Exploration* (New York: New York University, 1980), 4.

142 Ibid., 37.

143 Ibid., 5.

144 Ibid., 37.

145 Chute, 452.

146 Buckler, 38.

147 Michael Shallcross, *Rethinking G. K. Chesterton and Literary Modernism: Parody, Performance, and Popular Culture* (New York: Routledge, 2018), 3.

148 Ibid., 3.

149 Buckler, 37.

150 Chesterton, 89.

151 Ibid., 105.

152 Ibid., 106.

153 Ibid., 88.

154 Milbank, 34.

155 Ibid., 38.

156 Ibid., xv.

157 Neil Gaiman, *Sandman: The Wake* (New York: DC Comics, 1996), 81.

158 Milbank, 9.

159 Joan Gordon, "Prospero Framed in Neil Gaiman's *The Wake*," in *The Sandman Papers: An Exploration of the Sandman Mythology*, ed. Joseph L. Sanders (Seattle, WA: Fantagraphics, 2006), 81.

160 Castaldo, 103.

161 Round, 32.

162 Saxton, 22.

163 Katsiadas, 67.

164 For instance, Sarah Annes Brown notes how Gaiman's interests in the "relationship between the 'real' world and the worlds created in dream or fiction" are clear "in his imaginative responses to Shakespeare." Sarah Annes Brown, "'Shaping Fantasies': Responses to Shakespeare's Magic in Popular Culture," *Shakespeare*, 5, no. 2 (2009): 165, doi:10.1080/17450910902921591 (accessed October 19, 2021).

165 G. K. Chesterton, *Soul of Wit: G. K. Chesterton on William Shakespeare*, ed. Dale Ahlquist (Mineola: Dover Publications, 2012), 131, 133.

166 Ibid., 133.

167 Gaiman, *Sandman: Dream Country*, 74.

168 Ibid.

PROMETHEA THE HERMETIC IMAGINATION AND MODERN ENCHANTMENT

CHAPTER 2

"Imagination's blaze in mankind's dark": *Promethea*, the Hermetic Imagination, and Modern Enchantment

Recollecting

William Buckler describes how an "archetypal Romantic faith" persists in literary creativity from the early nineteenth century through the early twentieth century.[169] This faith is based on beliefs in the power of imaginative literature to elevate human integrity and drive human history. This faith takes various forms in mythologies that we find in the nineteenth and twentieth centuries, and I contend that it also takes various forms in mythologies that we find in modern comics. Reading these intersections creates space to explore comics' connections to larger, historically distinct discourses of which traditional literature is a part. In Chapter One, I use this framework to read Neil Gaiman's Romantic faith in the *Sandman* mythology, but this framework bears different consequences on Alan Moore and J. H. Williams III's *Promethea*. On one hand, Moore and Williams intersect with nineteenth-century myths in the ways that they use the *Promethea* mythology to convey personal ideas about imaginative literature's power to elevate human integrity. On the other hand, Moore and Williams do not connect their creativity to the literary imagination. Rather, their ideas are grounded in a different form of the imagination altogether: the hermetic imagination. This imaginative form is based on Kabbalist ideas about the ten *sefirot*—the divine emanations of the Judeo Christian God—and the Tree of Life. These differences do not undermine as much as they strengthen my argument that a greater Romantic literary history of comics exists. These differences become key to situating Moore and Williams in a diachronic Romantic literary history.

Early twentieth-century esoteric and occult movements understood the *sefirot* as divine emanations of God, also known as *Eyn-Sof* or a "Ruler" that is "absolutely undifferentiated in a complete and changeless unity."[170] These emanations comprise a metaphysical system known as the Tree of Life, and this system is illustrated by a symbol that conveys ideas about how divine energies descend into the material world (see Figure 3.1). In *Promethea*, Moore and Williams posit how the highest point in the material world, also known as *Malkuth*, is human imagination. The logic is that imagination

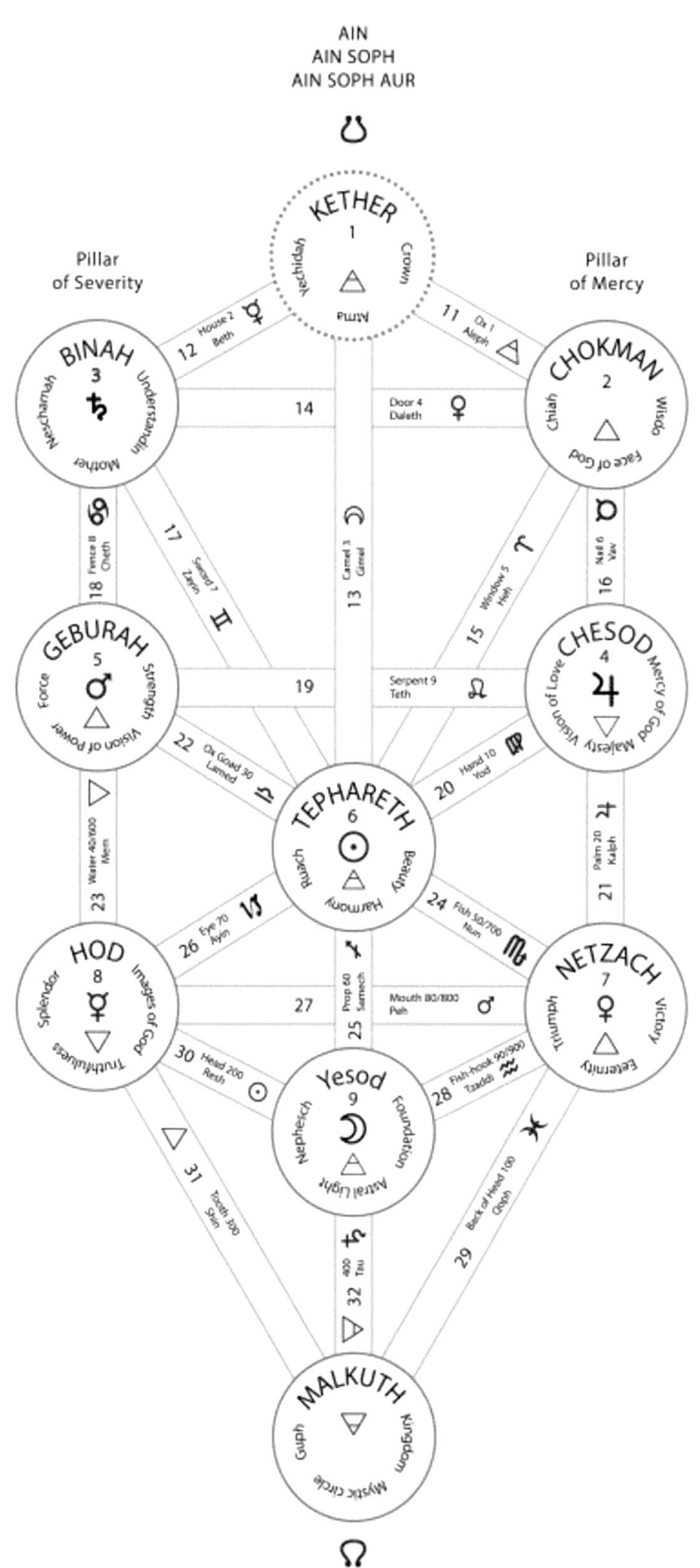

Fig. 3.1
The Tree of Life. Rabbi Nissan Dovid Dubov. *The Sefirot*. The Rohr Jewish Learning Institute, Accessed August 31, 2020. http://www.myjli.com/success/index.php/2016/11/30/the-sefirot/.

connects humankind to greater divine energies that descend from God. The drama of the story unfolds in how humankind is becoming more and more disconnected from sacred powers in an increasingly secular, postmodern society, and the heroic powers of art are needed to reconnect humankind to the divine. What is less obvious is that the hero of the story, Promethea, embodies a form of the imagination that can be traced from Moore and Williams to the early twentieth century and beyond to Romanticism. We are addressing another diachronic literary history of Romanticism, and the importance in this reading is at least threefold: It brings new insights to Moore and Williams's creative processes in *Promethea*; it indicates that a larger pattern of creativity in mainstream comics exists; and it expands the scope of comics' connections to larger literary projects that descend from Romanticism.

Promethea: New Foundations for Old Beliefs

Promethea follows the story of a young woman named Sophie Bangs, who discovers the ability to assume the persona of the mythical heroine Promethea while researching the figure for a college term paper. In the story, Promethea is the spirit of a little girl who "wanders into the imaginations" of artists who have "enough enthusiasm for the character,"[171] and she is needed throughout history to reconnect humankind to God. The artists who assume her identity achieve this function through the "magical" powers of storytelling.[172] Once their time on earth is finished, the artists take up residence in The Immateria, a space/place in the upper echelons of *Malkuth* (the tenth *sefirot* in the Tree of Life) from which all imaginative creativity emanates. The key to reading this story's place in Romantic literary history is the way that the character Promethea operates on two levels of narration. On one level, Sophie Bangs learns how to fulfill her heroic function by traveling through metaphysical realms within the Tree of Life, and on another level, Moore and Williams use the *Promethea* myth as a vehicle to explore their personal ideas about imaginative creativity's place within this larger system. The narrative highlights ideas that human history is contingent on the magical powers of artistic creativity, and this dynamic suggests that Moore and Williams construct their own creativity's relationship with the *Promethea* mythology. *Promethea* therefore becomes a personal mythology that the artists use to connect with an imaginative tradition, and their relationship with the story suggests that we can better understand not only Moore and Williams's artistic motives but also their place within Romantic literary history.

Criticism of *Promethea* has already addressed Moore's debt to Romanticism generally and to William Blake specifically. Tracee Howell, for instance, describes *Promethea* as "a tribute to magic in literary romanticism."[173] Roderick McGillis also explains that Moore's body of work "offers overt references to Blake, Shelley, and others," and he continues to examine the ways that Blake's "The Tyger" (see Figure 3.2) provides narrative structure in *Promethea*, *Watchmen*, and, among others, *Saga of the Swamp Thing*.[174] Such scholarship, however, gives little weight to the ways Moore and Williams draw upon ideas about magic from the occult and hermetic schools of thought, and these ideas concretize *Promethea*'s place in a diachronic Romantic literary history. The few comments about Moore and Williams's connections to the occult are grounded in ideas about their ambitions to rebel against the superhero genre. Howell describes *Promethea* as a "slippery hero-narrative in disguise."[175] Similarly, McGillis writes,

> [Promethea] appears at first glance to be a version of Wonder Woman; however, this Amazon is quite unlike Promethea. Promethea is not one but several women who take their place in various times. The implication is that Promethea is not an individual, but rather she is a function, or better yet, a state of mind...Douglas Wolk notes that the latest incarnation of Promethea, Sophie Bangs, can invoke the physical presence of the mythical heroine "by acts of imagination and creativity." "Imagination and creativity" invoke Romanticism in all its anti-Enlightenment glory.[176]

McGillis's and Howell's comments suggest that Moore and Williams initially lead readers to believe that they are going to experience a superhero narrative, but then deliberately extend the story into something else.

McGillis's ideas about Moore and Williams's initial efforts to connect *Promethea* to the superhero genre are grounded in *Promethea*'s iconography. Alex Romagnoli and Gian Pagnucci write about the superhero genre's symbolism: "[T]he emotions, values, and desires of the characters are usually embodied in a highly visual way. Captain America is the All-American superhero, so he wears a stylized American flag as his suit. This is blatant, but it is also effective for a medium, comics, that relies on the visuals to communicate."[177] These ideas about the genre's aesthetics suggest that J. H. Williams establishes a formal domain for readers before they even open the book by placing the visual representation of Promethea on the cover of the first issue. When readers pick up Williams's cover to *Promethea* No. 1, they see an image of the hero standing in a ray of white light, dressed in a golden breastplate, winged headband, and tassets decorated with an ankh. She is armed with a Caduceus and wears a cape as she gazes upward, drawing attention to her name, written in gold: PROMETHEA. The Egyptian god Thoth and the Greek god Hermes look upon her from either side, and her image splits two

The Tyger.

Tyger Tyger. burning bright,
In the forests of the night;
What immortal hand or eye.
Could frame thy fearful symmetry?

In what distant deeps or skies.
Burnt the fire of thine eyes?
On what wings dare he aspire?
What the hand, dare sieze the fire?

And what shoulder, & what art,
Could twist the sinews of thy heart?
And when thy heart began to beat,
What dread hand? & what dread feet?

What the hammer? what the chain,
In what furnace was thy brain?
What the anvil? what dread grasp,
Dare its deadly terrors clasp!

When the stars threw down their spears
And water'd heaven with their tears:
Did he smile his work to see?
Did he who made the Lamb make thee?

Tyger Tyger burning bright,
In the forests of the night:
What immortal hand or eye,
Dare frame thy fearful symmetry?

Fig. 3.2
William Blake's "The Tyger," from *The Songs of Innocence and Experience*. Image 31 from William Blake, *Songs of Innocence and of Experience, Shewing the Two Contrary States of the Human Soul* (London, W. Blake, 1794). Library of Congress, Lessing J. Rosenwald Collection, https://www.loc.gov/item/48031329/.

frames. One depicts Promethea as a little girl on a desert dune, and the other depicts Sophie Bangs cowering from a shadow creature. Attentive readers will recognize that Williams's cover is saturated in symbolism; it is textbook superhero iconography, from the gods overlooking the hero to the symbols from ancient mythologies and malevolent creatures. Right from the get-go, before readers open the book, Moore and Williams deliberately position them within a formal domain with certain expectations. What happens, however, is that the artists move Promethea from this formal domain into a space of "imagination and creativity," The Immateria. McGillis describes this space as resting on "what [Moore] might call 'magic,' the latter-day Romanticism of the Golden Dawn and Aleister Crowley."[178] Here, McGillis lays a critical foundation for exploring the series's concrete connections to larger literary projects of modernity that descend from Romanticism.

Promethea's connections to the Golden Dawn suggest that Moore and Williams's creativity becomes an extension of early twentieth-century efforts to revive Romanticism's ways of thinking about the human imagination and creativity. Michael Saler, for example, explains how early twentieth-century artists committed to artistic ideals of "reenchanting the world." Artists who functioned within this larger literary project sought to restore wonder and mystery to the human imagination during the rise of modern reason and secularism. One means of achieving reenchantment was to create "new myths compatible with rational and even secular outlooks."[179] Saler describes how, alongside science fiction and fantasy writers, "Turn of the century occult movements, new religions such as Christian Science, and adherents of more secular 'mind cure' strategies...highlighted the centrality of the imagination and its anterior worlds. They maintained that the imagination played a significant role in effecting both spiritual and somatic changes; for some, it even afforded access to existent 'Other-Worlds.'"[180] The importance that Moore and Williams place on magic and the imagination suggests that *Promethea* becomes an extension of this larger, ongoing creative project of modernity. Moore's comments about the series, in fact, recall this endeavor:

> Promethea raised some interesting ideas, particularly about current American culture, which seems to be about restricting ideas and the number of things that people can actually think about, in an almost Orwellian way. So we were saying, look, you don't have to be an atheist or a born-again Christian or a Muslim or in any other isolated and absolute position, but there is this huge palette of human possibilities that you can explore. It's probably a more constructive way to use your mind. It gives you a greater reverence for almost every aspect of existence. It's very similar to the Romantic position. William Blake was a Romantic, he was also an occultist and a visionary. It's all the same territory.[181]

Moore's comments not only capture a personal faith in the power of imaginative creativity to transform individuals, but they also describe an iconoclastic approach to myth-making that recalls Blake's position in *Jerusalem* about the will to "Create a System or be enslav'd by another Man's. / I will not Reason & Compare: my business is to Create."[182] In this vein, Moore and Williams intend *Promethea* to offer an alternative system of knowledge about the world—one that seeks to cultivate a "greater reverence for almost every aspect of existence." The idea energizing Moore and Williams's creativity is to exercise readers' imaginations, and their creative process reconceives the superhero genre as a vehicle to achieve these effects. They use the Promethea myth to teach readers their personal ideas about Kabbalah and the importance of the human imagination to elevate human integrity. This creative process situates *Promethea* as an extension of the project to reenchant the world in at least two ways: The artists centralize the hermetic imagination in the mythology, and their creative intent centralizes the belief in artistic creativity's role in spiritual change.

***Promethea* in Critical Context**

What becomes most important in concretizing Moore and Williams's connections to the *Promethea* mythology is how the distance between the hero and the artists closes: Moore and Williams literally become characters within the story. For example, in *Promethea: Book 3* (Issue 14), Sophie accesses the ninth *sefirah*, *Yesod*, by traveling through the Immateria. In this issue, a spread depicts Alan Moore shaking hands with J. H. Williams III. The logic is that artists transport themselves into spiritual realms through imagination.[183] Sophie says, "[*Yesod* is] a word, meaning Foundation. I guess it implies that spirituality is founded on imagination."[184] This closing of distance between Moore, Williams, and Promethea places the artists within the larger metaphysical system of The Tree of Life, and their roles as artists *in and out* of the story link their creativity to the ideals of the hermetic imagination that appear in the story: They intend to lead readers to higher spiritual realms and imaginative revelation. Opportunities arise, here, that allow us to trace this intent through literary history to the project of reenchantment and beyond—to the Romantic Period. We meet two difficulties, however, before we can place *Promethea* in this diachronic literary history of Romanticism.

The first difficulty is that prevailing criticism reads Promethea's journey through the Kabbalist Tree of Life as a postmodern rebellion against the superhero genre and its (alleged) limitations. Such criticism makes this claim by reading Promethea as a postmodern update to Percy Bysshe Shelley's titan Prometheus, from *Prometheus Unbound*. McGillis writes,

> Prometheus is one manifestation of the Romantic hero: strong, self-sacrificing, self-conscious, and fiercely independent…We see him as representative of victorious humanity in Shelley's *Prometheus Unbound*. In this great visionary work, Prometheus is the human form divine. What Moore and his collaborators, J. H. Williams III and Mick Gray, perform is a masterstroke of updating, making Prometheus female and undifferentiated…in what we might call a postmodern dance of selves.[185]

Here, McGillis's reading situates Prometheus as an archetype for the rebellious artist, and this reading recalls Geoffrey Hartman's description of the titan's narrative function in literary history: "To create a truly iconoclastic art, a structure-breaking art, to change the function of form from reconciliation and conservation to rebellion, and so to participate in the enormity of present experience—this is the one Promethean aim still fiery enough to inspire. It is the psychic state of art today."[186] McGillis extends this rebellious state of mind to Moore and Williams's Promethean character, and to be fair, it is logical. Since Moore's early 1980s debut in mainstream comics—with titles such as *Miracleman*, *V for Vendetta*, and *Saga of the Swamp Thing*—he and his creative teams have been notorious for creating stories that consciously deconstruct narrative conventions and carry artistic ambitions to show the greater potential of the superhero genre. The critical consensus is to read Moore's *œuvre* as a rebellion, but I maintain that artists are not required to function within one value system, nor are they required to be aesthetically consistent across an entire body of work.

A more productive line of inquiry with *Promethea* is to follow Moore and Williams's ways of using a Promethean figure as a vehicle to explore ideas about Kabbalah, magic, and imaginative storytelling. This line of inquiry builds on existing scholarship in and out of comics studies by helping us better understand not only *Promethea*'s connections to Romantic literary history, but also Romanticism's greater influence on later generations of artists. Saler, for example, explains how organizations, such as the Golden Dawn, emerged alongside various artistic responses to "secular trends of modernity" during the early twentieth century.[187] Charles Coulombe also argues that the hermetic imagination becomes "commonplace throughout fantasy literature. Exiled from mainstream Christian theology, academic philosophy, and the sciences, it has nevertheless subsisted, and even thrived."[188] Saler's and Coulombe's ideas suggest that contemporary artists become extensions of these literary traditions, and I take these ideas one step further by discussing how comics' place within the discourse of reenchantment remains almost completely unexplored in current scholarship. Certainly, there is room to explore how *Promethea*, specifically, and comics, generally, are connected to this creative project, but not coincidentally, it is also here where we meet the second difficulty in grounding *Promethea* in prior literary traditions: The critical consensus is that Moore and Williams consciously resist literary-historical inquiries.

Current scholarship is wont to read Moore's body of work as a rebellion against not only genre but also modes of interpretation. Howell prefaces her discussion of *Promethea* as a series where literary scholars' "traditional analytical tools, our steely knives of cold logic, our sure foundations of genre and disciplinary fields, our technical terminologies, may be of little use."[189] Howell's ideas emerge from the ways Moore and Williams deliberately detach the *Promethea* narrative from literary history by fabricating a literary tradition, and a good way to understand this fabrication is to compare the series, briefly, to *Sandman* and *The Unwritten*. For example, in *Sandman*, Gaiman uses Morpheus as a vehicle to reimagine William Shakespeare's literary career, and in *The Unwritten*, Carey and Gross use the mythical figure of Leviathan to reimagine the history of storytelling, from the *Epic of Gilgamesh* up through J. R. R. Tolkien, C. S. Lewis, and their Inkling circle. In short, Gaiman and Carey and Gross concretely connect their mythologies to historically based literary elements. The difficulty with *Promethea* is that Moore and Williams construct a literary genealogy for the mythical heroine that has no roots in actual literary history, and the critical discourse suggests that this narrative activity prevents us from grounding the story in literary history.

For instance, Moore's preface to *Book 1*, titled "The Promethea Puzzle: An Adventure in Folklore,"[190] details what appears to be a scholarly account of Promethea's literary history. It begins by recollecting Promethea's first alleged appearance in a late eighteenth-century fairy tale by Charlton Sennet: "[S]ome fifty lines into his epic sentimental fantasy *A Faerie Romance*, New England poet Charlton Sennet (1751–1803) makes his first mention of a character [Promethea] who has since then evolved into a fascinating literary mystery in her own right."[191] Moore continues to trace the character's literary history up through various imaginative traditions, including newspaper comic strips, pulp fiction, and comic books, until the trail disappears. He ends the preface and signs his name:

> So today, Promethea is in limbo—or perhaps Misty Magic Land—with her adventures no longer before the public. Given the popularity of simplistic post-modern characters such as the inexplicably celebrated Weeping Gorilla, perhaps it's simply that times have moved on, and that there is no longer a place for the romantic fantasy and play of the imagination that Promethea represents. We can only hope that she is merely resting in some corner of the Realm of Faerie, or of Hy Brasil, and that in the future, she'll turn up in a new guise, some fresh twist to her puzzling history, a genuine piece of American folklore in action, of poetry in motion.
>
> —Alan Moore.[192]

What seems to be a detailed literary history of Promethea is, in fact, part of the fiction. The texts in which Promethea allegedly appears and the artists who create stories about her are no more real than the fictional characters in the story itself. The critical consensus is that the preface is a false document, and the logic is that *Promethea* resists literary-historical approaches that comparatively explore influence, response, intertextuality, adaptation, appropriation—call it what you will.

The difficulty in pursuing *Promethea*'s literary history rests in how prevailing criticism reads the series's preface as a Moorean activity that challenges artistic and scholarly communities through narrative deconstruction and misdirection. Howell reads the preface as Moore's "vital critique" of postmodernism's influences on academic culture and artistic creativity:

> [It] reads like academic prose, like a professorial account that both provides a helpful overview of Promethea's impact on literary culture and bemoans the loss of this mythic figure in current fiction...In placing himself there, as a character mourning the loss of real meaning amongst postmodern literary culture, Moore at once satirizes the postmodern and destabilizes the same universalist meaning that twentieth-century postmodern approaches to textual study sought to challenge.[193]

Here, Howell suggests that Moore uses the preface in at least three ways: He misdirects readers from common reading strategies, such as comparative studies with source-texts, and he uses it to critique, simultaneously, postmodern ideas about the impossibility of shared meaning as well as ideas about the possibility of shared meaning. It is in these ways, she argues, that Moore and Williams exert control over how readers experience the text and perceive meaning in it.

Howell concludes that *Promethea* is a "monstrous" text that "in [Jeffrey Jerome] Cohen's words 'quite literally incorporates fear, desire, anxiety, and fantasy.'"[194] In this framework, the text resists the kinds of critical reading strategies that typically lead to better understandings of texts. The logic is that academic readers experience fear, desire, anxiety, and fantasy from this lack of control, and she concludes that *Promethea* encourages us to "abandon all boundaries, to dissolve categorization and read with *différance*."[195] In other words, the text allegedly encourages us to submit to the proliferation of meaning, to the impossibility of shared meaning, and to Moore and Williams's "monster" that "resists any one critical approach or univocalist reading."[196]

An alternative to Howell's ideas about the "monstrous" and *différance* is to examine Moore and Williams's process of citing and translating the Promethea mythology within the preface and throughout the story. In this framework, their creative process energizes the growth of meaning for readers. Instead of *différance*, Jacques Derrida's ideas about myth and translation help us reread *Promethea* without the fear and anxiety of the monstrous. This framework suggests that Moore and Williams grow the Promethea myth by creating an imagined literary history and translating the character into different genres, time periods, and artistic mediums. In doing so, Moore and Williams create an imaginative versatility from which they can draw certain aesthetics, and these aesthetics help develop their ideas about imaginative creativity's redeeming characteristics. If there is one idea around which the narrative revolves, it is that the world is in need of heroic imaginative creativity, and Promethea is its savior: "The world is our systems, our politics, our economies...our *ideas* of the world...Promethea is imagination... War, all war and conflict, is naught but the failure of imagination."[197] Instead of the deferral of meaning, *Promethea*'s preface begins an ongoing growth of shared meaning.

***Promethea*: A Holy Growth of Myth**

The key to better understanding Moore and Williams's process of growing the Promethea myth rests in following how they transfer the story from the superhero genre into a realm of the sacred—into the formal domain of Kabbalah. Derrida, for instance, explains that a myth offers itself to translation for a "holy growth" of its language and meaning.[198] He writes, "The sacred text assigns the task to the translator, and it is sacred *inasmuch as* it announces itself as transferable, simply transferable, to-be-translated."[199] This framework suggests that *Promethea*'s preface announces how the story translates into different genres, mediums, and time periods. The preface becomes a source of translation, and Moore and Williams engage an ongoing process of developing the meanings that the myth carries throughout their storytelling. To borrow Derrida's words, Moore and Williams "surrender" the text to translation, and it "devotes itself to the sacred."[200] In this way, readers follow how Moore and Williams generate meaning, and the artists devote the myth to the hermetic imagination's sacred space.

My framework suggests that *Promethea*'s formal aesthetics do not resist literary-historical approaches as much as they demand critical engagement with the hermetic imagination. Howell suggests that Moore and Williams move the story from the domain of superhero fiction and into something else that cannot be traced: "the stuff of human imagination and creativity itself."[201] Wolk characterizes *Promethea*'s "extended explanation of the Kabbala's [*sic*] Tree of Life" as "a lot of ungainly expository dialogue."[202] However, such scholarship indicates that it has all but ignored reading this imaginative form in context with Romantic literary history. Derrida's framework for reading the growth of myth provides a way of reading Moore and Williams's process of extending the Promethea myth into a sacred domain, and this domain is traceable through literary history to Romanticism. This line of inquiry creates opportunity to trace

Moore and Williams's connections to the early twentieth-century literary history of which the hermetic imagination is a part: the reenchantment of the world. The importance in understanding this literary history rests in how it provides a means to reread and better understand how Christian esotericism and occultism pour over into late twentieth- and twenty-first-century comics creativity.

We can locate *Promethea*'s literary history within the larger history of the Romantic movement by slow, patient historical method. This framework requires that we cover details about the hermetic imagination's place in literary history and the historical conditions from which it emerged. Saler's ideas about contemporary imaginary worlds are a good starting point, because Moore and Williams invent The Immateria and construct this imaginary place in the Tree of Life. Saler's framework provides context for this imaginary space and the artistic motives energizing its creativity. His main discussion is driven by the idea that contemporary fantasy writers engage in forms of creativity that were first energized by the "'big bang' of imaginary worlds [that] flared into existence" at the turn of the twentieth century.[203] It is during this time, he explains, that burgeoning scientific fields and perspectives of the natural world, such as evolutionary biology and psychoanalysis, began to take a large hold on Western culture. Saler's co-author, Joshua Landy, characterizes this shift as a move to a reason-based culture. Landy writes,

> At one time we considered rainbows mysterious phenomena, divine perhaps in origin (Iris's scarf, God's covenant), but then science came along and taught us about prismatic refraction. We used to believe that the cosmos had—as its etymology suggests—an intrinsic, humanly apprehensible order, with the earth firmly set at its center; after Copernicus, we thought differently. And though we fondly imagined for a while that we were placed on earth for a purpose, we now know that our evolution involved a considerable degree of contingency, and might just as well not have happened at all.[204]

Landy and Saler argue that empirical sciences and reason demystified, secularized, disillusioned—in a word, "disenchanted"—much of the Western world's sense of mystery and wonder. The twentieth century saw a new sense of Enlightenment begin to occupy the human mind where religion and myth once dwelled.

Saler and Landy's ideas about "disenchantment" describe a collective state of mind that has a "God-shaped void."[205] Saler, however, argues that artists sought to compensate for this void: "The modern West has been called 'disenchanted,' but that is a half-truth. It can be equally deemed an enchanted place, in which imaginary worlds and fictional characters have replaced the sacred groves and tutelary deities of the premodern world."[206] Here, Saler begins to explain that early twentieth-century fantasy writers became part of a larger reactionary discourse to modernity's alleged disenchantment, and we find that many artists during this time period committed to ideals of compensating for this experience through imaginary world-building. This argument suggests that secular art and its images and symbols began to populate the human imagination and become just as important to human experience as mythical and religious figures of the past. Imaginary worlds, such as J. R. R. Tolkien's Middle-earth and H. P. Lovecraft's Cthulhu mythos, reconciled empirical science with imagination, and Saler suggests that these worlds invited readers to accompany fictional characters, often highly idyllic, throughout their journeys. Artists intended readerly experiences to become imaginative exercises that facilitate intellectual transfers from readers' understandings of fictional worlds to their understandings of the real world.

Within Saler's framework, popular imaginary worlds in the literary marketplace became tools of communication, sociability, and reenchantment. The logic follows how readers participated in larger "discussions about imaginary worlds [that] often segued into discussions about the real world. Public spheres of the imagination provided playful spaces in which controversial views about society were debated critically yet with mutual respect."[207] For instance, these spheres of imagination "could help their visitors realize that something as seemingly natural as the nation...was in important respects an 'imagined community' brought to life through many of the same social mechanisms used to maintain the virtual existence of Middle-earth or the Starfleet Federation."[208] Here, the idea is that the details in secular imaginary worlds encourage communities of readers to question the validity of characters' sociocultural and sociohistorical experiences within imaginary worlds, for instance, the cultural differences between the Rohirrim and the Men of Gondor in Tolkien's work—and these nations' differences from the societies of elves and dwarves. Each nation and community of Middle-earth has a history and set of beliefs that extend from the creation of "Arda," or Earth. Readers can better understand, for example, the hostility between dwarves and elves during the events of *The Lord of the Rings* by reading about the *Nauglamír* and the Battle of the Thousand Caves during the First Age of Middle-earth. Saler's framework suggests that Tolkien fans become "reenchanted" by discussing the historical and cultural dynamics of Middle-earth, and the logic is that such reading strategies lead readers to realize the historical and cultural intricacies of the real world and their place within it. Saler and Landy tend to focus on fantasy and science fiction writers' responses to the secular trends of modernity, but they also touch on how this sense of artistic responsibility to reenchant modernity poured over into various creative activities during the early twentieth century, including Christian esotericism and occult movements to which *Promethea* is connected.

Along with his discussion of the enchantments of science fiction and fantasy, Saler briefly addresses alternative forms of the imagination and reenchantment that emerged at the turn of the twentieth century. While the popular literary marketplace invited readers to inhabit multiple imaginary worlds, the occult invited readers to explore metaphysical worlds from Kabbalah and tarot, and forms of ritual "magic" gained popularity. These religious models offered alternative practices for reenchantment that were not offered by the "scientific and secular trends" of the early twentieth century.[209] Western occult movements, such as the Hermetic Order of the Golden Dawn and Helena Blavatsky's Theosophical Society, emerged alongside fantasy writers as allies in the project of reenchantment. With as much zeal as fantasy writers, members of these societies pushed against disenchantment and promoted a world full of meaning, wonder, and power. The logic of the hermetic imagination, for example, follows how such meaning may become intelligible through the "growth of expansion of consciousness by way of symbolic modalities."[210] In other words, the hermetic world view promoted ideas about the ways the material world is full of symbols that conceal higher planes of reality, and these higher realities could be accessed by practicing elaborate symbolic interpretations of sacred texts, which became known as "magick."

The twentieth-century hermetic imagination elevates ideas about the ways words and images contain mystical powers that can make higher realities intelligible, and we find these exact ideas within *Promethea*. Such reservoirs of knowledge provided early twentieth-century artists an imaginative plenitude from which to draw and construct personal symbolic systems, such as W. B. Yeats's work in *A Vision*. Charles Coulombe explains that the hermetic imagination endures in the work of artists who inherited literature from Yeats, Maude Gonne, Arthur Machen, and Charles Williams. These authors' worldviews, he argues, have now "come to be commonplace throughout fantasy literature."[211] It is well documented that these writers, Yeats in particular, inherited Victorian and Romantic forms of imagination.[212] We also see these writers maintain the Romantic image of the artist in the figure of the magician. In the hermetic worldview, the magician is synonymous with the artist, and this figure bears the responsibility of wielding the creative powers of the mind. We can take Saler's and Coulombe's ideas further by examining how the hermetic imagination persists through comics creativity. Their ideas suggest that Moore and Williams's formal domain in *Promethea* descends from this imaginative form.

Promethea, Romanticism, and the Golden Dawn

Saler's focus on the social efficacy of imaginary worlds and Coulombe's interest in the hermetic imagination's endurance give weight to the idea that reenchantment is an ongoing project of modernity, and their frameworks suggest that Moore and Williams's *Promethea* is an extension of it. We can advance both sets of ideas by better understanding the Romantic literary history of the hermetic imagination, and we can achieve this better understanding by tracing *Promethea*'s literary history to Romanticism's earlier age of disenchantment. As we saw in the Introduction and Chapter One of this book, William Buckler offers one way to trace the "archetypal Romantic faith" in imaginative creativity from our contemporary moment to the early nineteenth century.[213] Buckler's ideas created opportunities to ground how Gaiman, Moore and Williams, and Carey and Gross invent mythologies based on this essential faith.

Edmund Wilson offers another way to understand how Romantic faith energized the work of nineteenth- and twentieth-century artists. Wilson specifically focuses W. B. Yeats's connections to the occult and how he "frequented clairvoyants and students of Astrology and Magic."[214] Yeats's interests in these ways of thinking eventually led him to create an "elaborate mystical-metaphysical system" in *A Vision*.[215] This system is based on Yeats's associations with the Golden Dawn, and it provides a great model against which we can compare Moore and Williams's ways of thinking about "magic" in *Promethea*. In *A Vision*, Yeats invents a hermetic system, demands that readers cooperate and follow his personal vision of this system, and uses it to ascribe new meanings and importance to the world. Such "ultra-Romantic effects"[216] on readers depend on Yeats's ideas about the sacred powers of the imagination and its place in a larger metaphysical system.

It is important to understand, with some certainty, how Romantic faith is part and parcel of the hermetic imagination's literary history before reading Moore and Williams's personal version of it in *Promethea*. Yeats's system in *A Vision* is a helpful comparative model for constructing this critical framework. Wilson, for example, begins his discussion of Yeats's connections to the occult in relation to a group of "Romantics who, in certain ways, carried Romanticism further" than the Romantics themselves: the French Symbolists.[217] He explains that the rigor of the Romantic age—its poetic declarations and its revolutionary energy—found its way into their work in the late nineteenth century. The emergence of the Symbolists and their influences on early twentieth-century creativity complement Saler's ideas about the ways writers who were connected to the occult embraced the imagination and made compatible "the spiritual with [the] secular."[218] However, where Saler argues that fantasy writers in this period "freed [themselves] from the religious and utilitarian strictures of Coleridge's era,"[219] Wilson's focus on aesthetics is helpful to better understand the persistence of Romanticism through the Symbolists, to Yeats,[220] and up through our contemporary moment.

Wilson expands on his ideas about the historical context of the Symbolists and the persistence of their ideas when describing how they drew from Romantic aesthetics. He writes, "[A] language must make use of symbols: what is so special, so fleeting and so vague cannot be conveyed by direct statement or descriptions, but only by succession of words, of images, which will serve to suggest it to the reader. The symbolists themselves, full of the idea of producing with poetry effects like those of music, tended to think of these images as possessing an abstract value like musical notes and chords."[221] Here, Wilson explains that the Symbolists understood poetry as playing upon readers' imaginations just as musical frequencies play upon an individual's sense of sound. This idea of the acoustic image is rooted in Romantic conceptions about the ways words and images impress upon the human mind. The Romantics energized certain ways of thinking about symbolism's effects on human experiences with art, and the Symbolists inherited these doctrines from Romanticism. Romanticism then persisted up through the Modernists, who were "instructed" in Symbolist doctrines and ways of thinking about artistic creativity.[222]

Yeats's involvement with the Golden Dawn is well documented, and his ideas about artistic responsibility and artistic efficacy help us better understand Romanticism's movement from the early nineteenth century, up through the Symbolists, into the early twentieth-century hermetic imagination, and into our contemporary moment. Coulombe writes, "For Yeats Magic and Poetry were near synonymous...Whether he was dealing with fairy-lore or mystic visions, the conviction that this world both symbolises [*sic*] and conceals greater realities was ever obvious in his work."[223] Yeats believed that it is the artist's responsibility to use images and symbols to reveal "greater realities" and "reintegrate the Christian Mysteries into Man's Art and conception of reality."[224] This sense of artistic purpose energizes his work in *A Vision*, and this purpose places Yeats in the larger, historically distinct project to reenchant the world by restoring wonder and mystery to humankind. He constructs an elaborate metaphysical system with geometric shapes and artistic images, and he intends to perform "magic" by leading readers to rethink their purpose within a larger metaphysical system.

Yeats's ideas about the artist's responsibilities to perform "magic" are put into practice in the creation of *A Vision*. According to Neil Mann, the hermetic ideas about magic from which Yeats draws "[make] philosophy and doctrine into drama and symbol in order to create ceremony."[225] Yeats's philosophy, in other words, is concerned with an artistic ceremony that raises one's consciousness by invoking images and symbols that act upon the human mind, and he commits to these ideas in his creativity. Similarly, Moore and Williams's *Promethea* draws attention to ideas about elevating people's consciousness through the "magic" of imaginative creativity, and the artists' presence in the narrative suggests that they commit to these ways of thinking. An important distinction between *A Vision* and *Promethea*, however, is that Yeats invents a new system from preexisting systems, while Moore and Williams explore ideas in preexisting systems, including Kabbalah, tarot, and (among others) astrology.

On one hand, Yeats's ways of thinking about magic and creativity in *A Vision* become organized according to a larger structural system that he invents. This system is "worked out with geometrical diagrams and set forth in terms of such unfamiliar conceptions as *daimons, tinctures, cones, gyres, husks and passionate bodies*."[226] On the other hand, *Promethea* is an invented myth, but it is more a superhero narrative than the invention of a new metaphysical system; the character's journey through the paths of the ten *sefirot* is structured by systems that were already there to explore. This difference does not pose a problem as much as it helps us read and better understand Moore and Williams' creative process. Moore and Williams intersect with Yeats in drawing from the hermetic imagination, and they extend superhero conventions to Kabbalist and tarot systems. Not only do Moore and Williams extend the formal domains of superhero narratives into the hermetic imagination, but the artists' motives for moving into new formal domains connect with the ideas of reenchantment.

Yeats, for example, becomes attached to the project of reenchantment in his ideas about magic and the "mystical life." Yeats writes,

> Now as to Magic. It is surely absurd to hold me 'weak' or otherwise because I chose to persist in a study which I decided deliberately four or five years ago to make, next to my Poetry, the most important pursuit of my life. Whether it be, or be not, bad for my health can only be decided by one who knows what Magic is and not at all by any amateur. If I had not made Magic my constant study I could not have written a single word of my Blake book, nor would *The Countess Kathleen* have ever come to exist. The Mystical life is the centre [*sic*] of all that I do and all that I think and all that I write.[227]

Here, Yeats defends his interests in magic against both secular trends and orthodox Christianity. Much like William Blake's refusal to be "enslaved by another man's" system, Yeats proclaims that he "knew a Christian's ecstasy without his slavery to custom."[228] My point is that Yeats's "mystical life" is based on a religious freedom, and it intersects with the ideas driving Moore's creative process: "[W]e were saying, look, you don't have to be an atheist or a born-again Christian or a Muslim or in any other isolated and absolute position, but there is a huge palette of human possibilities that you can explore."[229] Moore and Williams's intersections with Yeats do not stop there. They draw from the Golden Dawn's ideas about the importance of imagination, and they subscribe to the Romantic image of the artist-as-magician. The magician, or "magus," assumes responsibilities to practice magic through the creation of artistic symbols, and Moore and Williams's relationship with the Promethea myth suggests that the character is a personal archetype. As Promethea redeems humankind in the story through magical powers of the imagination, Moore and Williams intend *Promethea* to play upon readers' imaginations and play a role in redeeming the real world—the reader's world.

Imagination and Magical Incantation in *Promethea*

Throughout *Promethea*, Moore and Williams engage in an ongoing translation of the Promethea mythology, and this activity constructs a formal space of imaginative plenitude. This space is also energized by the idea that artistic images and symbols contain mystical powers that connect humankind to divine energies. Kabbalah, to borrow Coulombe's words, "suggests a world of meaning,"[230] and meaning in *Promethea* is generated by a faith in art's "magical" capabilities to awaken humankind to larger metaphysical systems and our place in them. Saler's ideas about the occult's place in reenchanting modernity take Coulombe's ideas one step further, and their ways of thinking suggest that Moore and Williams's *Promethea* is an extension of a larger literary project descended from Romanticism. The artists inhabit a narrative in which artists assume the responsibilities of "magicians," and these responsibilities include raising readers' consciousnesses and ascribing new meaning to their worlds. A key to understanding Moore and Williams's connections to this literary history rests in their inhabitation of the story and their ways of thinking about artists as magicians. The magician, therefore, becomes Moore and Williams's personal archetype of artists within *Promethea*. Not only are Moore and Williams engaged in artistic creativity *while writing about* how artists wield magical powers of artistic creativity, but they also write and draw themselves into the story as artists accessing higher realms in the Tree of Life. The artists' inhabitation of the narrative situates them as being committed to the rules that they establish in the narrative; they submit to artists' roles in the Promethea mythology's larger hermetic system.

Moore and Williams base their artistic identity on the figure of the magician, and this reading brings new insights to comics' connections to a greater literary history extending from Romanticism. In *Promethea*, Moore and Williams position artists as wielding magical powers of imagination. They highlight this idea when Promethea journeys into "magic…where thoughts parade in fancy dress upon the state of consciousness."[231] This "parade" takes the form of a deck of tarot cards, and the twin snakes to Promethea's caduceus guide her through the symbolism of each one. They introduce themselves as "Mike" and "Mack"—for "microcosm" and "macrocosm"—and explain each card's symbolic meanings. Mike begins, "I'm Mike, he's Mack. One's front, the other's back. These are the mind's high halls, dear child, with golden information tiled. Here is revealed, for all to see, the magic of reality." Mack answers, "Conversely, we may also view reality in magic, too. The universe's starry rash that burst from nowhere in a flash, the magic of this earthly ball, the wonder that we're here at all!"[232] Upon reaching Card One, the Magician's card, Mike and Mack explain what this figure represents:

> The Fool to the Magician wields,
> And from the vacant quantum fields erupts the singularity
> Of all that is, or that may be.
> The Magus represents the will
> That made things happen, then, and still…
> He's every artist, scribe or sage.
> 'Tis he that marks the empty page.
> He is whichever seems least odd:
> A Big Bang, or a Father God.[233]

Here, Moore and Williams establish the idea that artists become godlike in acts of creativity. They practice "magic" by calling forth into being *something* out of *nothing*, and their artistic images and symbols impress upon readers' minds. In the story, artistic images and symbols create new meaning in one's life and one's understanding of reality, and this framework suggests that Moore and Williams take ownership of their own artistic images and symbols by inhabiting the narrative.

Moore and Williams's appearance as artists in *Promethea* suggests that they position themselves as magicians tapping into spiritual realms by way of imaginative exercises. This specularity suggests that Moore and Williams commit to the rules of the myth. As artists writing a *Promethea* story, they intend to "perform magic" by invoking the image of Promethea and exploring Kabbalah. Throughout the series, Moore and Williams explore tarot and astrology, and they dedicate eleven total chapters to exploring the ten *sefirot* and the "invisible" sphere, named *Daath*, in the Kabbalist Tree of Life.[234] It is in this way that the plot complements the artists' ideals to perform magic and awaken readers to truths and existences beyond the material world. In the final issue (Issue 32, Volume 5), Promethea addresses the readers, and her comments explicitly define these ideals:

> *Promethea*, like everything you've ever read or witnessed, is made only of light: The reflected light of this poster-comic playing over your eye. The light of imagination and play of meaning across your mind...Imagination can transform us. Yesod, the lunar sphere of imagination, is the foundation on which our spiritual life rests. Imagination arises out of consciousness, which itself blossoms from Hod, the mercurial, magical sphere of language...Using language, imagination, and will, we create reality, moment by moment, weaving concepts and sensations, light and sound, on the loom of our consciousness...just as you're doing now, reading this final episode of *Promethea*.[235]

Promethea's remarks suggest that Moore and Williams intend to use language, imagination, and will to create meaning and raise readers' consciousnesses through imagination and creativity—through magical incantation. I have demonstrated how these artistic ideals can be traced from *Promethea* to larger literary traditions that energized the hermetic imagination of the Golden Dawn, but how these ideals play out in my framework challenges current understandings of the story.

In *Promethea*, Sophie Bangs discovers that Promethea's responsibility is to energize an apocalypse, and the difficulty we meet with current scholarship is that it already understands Moore and Williams's vision of apocalypse in the context of Romanticism. McGillis, for example, reads Moore's body of work with "darker" visions of Romantic apocalypse. He writes,

> Romanticism is an end time state of mind. It takes an interest in apocalyptic vision, but a particular kind of apocalyptic vision...The Romantic apocalypse delivers a vision of a renewed earth, a marriage of Heaven and Hell, a release of Promethean energies in an epithalamion such as we have in act 4 of Shelley's *Prometheus Unbound*....But another side of this vision exists, a dark Romantic apocalypse seen in a poem such as [Lord] Byron's "Prometheus" or in Mary Shelley's novel, *The Last Man*. This secular vision is less optimistic than the work touched by the euphoria of July 14, 1789; it reflects the pessimism rising from the failure of that revolution. This inverted apocalypse informs our contemporary sense of the end times, and Moore's work shares more with this vision than it does with the ecstatic visions of the Romantic renovated earth.[236]

Here, McGillis suggests that *Watchmen*, *V for Vendetta*, and *Promethea* use an inverted model of Romanticism's celebratory visions of apocalypse. To McGillis's credit, he is right to comparatively examine Moore's and Byron's Promethean characters, but the apocalyptic vision from Byron best suited to compare *Watchmen* and *V for Vendetta* is "Darkness." When writing his poem "Prometheus," an exiled Byron used myth to create an autobiographical simile with the titan's exile on Caucasus, whereas "Darkness" paints a bleak, apocalyptic vision:

The world was void,
The populous and the powerful was a lump,
Seasonless, herbless, treeless, manless, lifeless—
A lump of death—a chaos of hard clay.[237]

Moore's apocalyptic visions in *V for Vendetta* and *Watchmen* bear distinct connections to Byron's aesthetics of human destruction, division, death, and despair. *Promethea*, however, bears more in common with what M. H. Abrams addresses as an apocalypse by "revolution of consciousness,"[238] not destruction and decay. He writes, "[F]aith in an apocalypse by revelation had been replaced by faith in an apocalypse by revolution, and this now gave way to faith in an apocalypse by imagination or cognition."[239] This apocalypse by imagination envisions a restored unity and a renovated reality through an awakening of the human psyche, and we find this form of imagination in *Promethea*. Rather than recalling Byronic pessimism and despair, Moore and Williams's ideas about imaginative revelation recall Shelley's idealism in *Prometheus Unbound*:

[All] That tempers or improves man's life, now free.
And lovely apparitions, dim at first,
Then radiant—as the mind, arising bright
From the embrace of beauty.[240]

Moore and Williams have more in common with this vision of apocalypse in *Promethea*.

For example, Sophie asks a prior version of Promethea, the newspaper cartoonist Margaret Case, if an apocalypse is a bad thing: "Uhh, but…the end of the world. That's a bad thing, right?" Case responds, "Is it? 'The world' isn't the planet or life and people on it. The world is our systems, our politics, our economies…our *ideas* of the world! It's our flags and our banknotes and our border wars. I was at Ypres. I was at the Somme. I say end this filthy mess *now*."[241] Here, Moore and Williams encourage readers to think about apocalypse not in physical terms—as in the mass destruction, chaos, and genocide that we see in *V for Vendetta* and *Watchmen*—but in terms of imaginative revelation. Case continues, "We have many names for this event. We call it 'The Rapture.' We call it 'The Opening of the 32nd Path.' We call it the *Awakening*, or the *Revelation*, or the *Apocalypse*. But 'End of the World' will do."[242]

The revolution of consciousness that occurs in *Promethea* works on two narrative levels. On one level, *Promethea*'s foundations rest on the artists' ideas about magic and the Kabbalist system of the Tree of Life, and this system becomes a landscape of artistic images through which the character Promethea navigates—from the material world, known as *Malkuth*, to the Godhead, known as *Kether*. When Sophie returns from *Kether*, she ends the world. In this apocalypse, people remember that "each brick, each busted tail-light in this mad stampede of world and time was Holy, to be loved,"[243] and they recognize "something shining under the familiar crease and contour of our faces, this unique light of our mythical being, our holy personalities."[244] It is important to reread these effects of Promethea's act of revelation in context with Shelley's idealism rather than Byron's pessimism, because it leads to better and more accurate understandings of the story's literary history. In the story, Promethea reconnects humankind to the divine. She regenerates humankind's relationship with the sacred world through the apocalypse of imagination.

On another level, Promethea's "magical" activities in the story connect Moore and Williams to the artistic motive for imaginative revelation. They connect with the artistic ideals of *Promethea* by intending the story to be pedagogical. *Promethea* becomes, in Moore's own words, a "protracted rant on magic."[245] For example, in *Book 3*, Sophie-as-Promethea leaves the earthly, material world to find her friend Barbara, and she takes the path to *Yesod*. She proceeds through the ten *sefirot*, or divine emanations, in preparation for her final act of revelation. Wolk characterizes this journey as something that does not intend "to tell a story so much as to present a gigantic mass of arcane philosophy as entertainingly and memorably as possible."[246] What I add to this dynamic is that the hermetic imagination's literary history suggests that Moore and Williams use the narrative to tell a story and also teach their audience about the Kabbalist system. The exposition is not "ungainly"[247] as much as it becomes a pedagogical exercise through which readers learn about Kabbalah and its ways of viewing the world. Moore and Williams encourage readers to experience a new, different way of thinking about the world—a world not devoid of meaning but saturated in it.

In *Promethea*, the collaborative dynamics of image and text—artist and writer—facilitate a distinct and deliberate aesthetic experience intended to teach. Readers follow Sophie on her journey to *Kether*, and when entering each *sefirot*, she and her companions explain the symbols that they find and the meanings they convey; characters act as spokespeople for the artists, and the visual images complement the larger structure and intent of the series. For example, Sophie and Barbara advance into the seventh *sefirah*, called

Netzach, and this space/place is pervaded by images and text that are metaphorical vehicles. *Netzach* is the realm of emotion, and Sophie interprets the landscape for Barbara while, at the same time, interpreting the page's symbolic images for readers. "It's emotion. Water is emotion, its element," Sophie says as they submerge into what appears to be water on a physical level but is "water on a *symbolic* level, water as a symbol of *emotion*."[248] As they reemerge, Barbara comments, "God, that was a strange experience, being dragged and thrown around by moods and feelings…but maybe that's just life." And Sophie responds, "Yeah. It makes you wonder if we have emotions or if emotions have us."[249] In a similar way, when they reach the *sefirah* named *Kether*, otherwise known as the Supreme Crown and the Godhead, the realm is saturated with white and gold images of various moments in time, space, and mind. Barbara explains the *sefirah*'s meaning: "*Kether*, the Crown. Here in the first white spark of being…God is everything. Everything is God. God is all. All One. All God. All *Kether*. One perfect moment, when everything happens. Always like this. The white brilliance. The bay leaf and ambergris. Here we are again."[250] The logic is that the physical and metaphysical realms in the Tree of Life are emanations from God's "first white spark of being." As Sophie and Barbara journey through the *sefirot*, Moore and Williams invite readers to better understand Kabbalah, and in *Kether*, they encourage readers to understand and read their worldly experiences as sacred experiences.

Promethea's pedagogical dynamics are defined by Moore and Williams's personal vision of Kabbalah, and this vision is based on artistic ideals of liberating the human mind from the world's existing systems and restoring meaning to the world. Moore and Williams dramatize these ideals through the narrative ideas about "magic" and artistic creativity's capabilities to raise readers' consciousnesses. In an interview with George Khoury, Moore comments,

> I've always believed that if you could write something intelligent in plain language, then that will raise people's consciousness. You can give them an idea that they may not have already had. If you write in a form that they can understand and comprehend and accept. Then you may be, instead of producing a generation of morons as your audience, you might be able to wake people up a bit, raise their expectations, get them to demand more intelligent fare. Get them to actually realize that they have a right to intelligent material. Which I think would be good for everybody. If that were the case, if people were a little bit more demanding. If they didn't just reward the same formulaic pap over and over again with their attention.[251]

Prevailing criticism situates *Promethea* as resistant to literary-historical inquiries, but Moore's comments suggest that he and

Williams's artistic motives were energized by Romantic faith in imaginative literature. Whether drawing from pagan mythology, hermetic lore, Kabbalah, Christianity, Neoplatonism, or any number of symbolic systems, Romantic writers and succeeding generations use larger systems to elevate ideas about the ways literature and the arts are powerful forces contributing to humankind's progress. Such models of history are defined by their ideas of a progressive movement toward an ideal of human perfection, whether this ideal be the recovery of an Edenic state of being, a reunion with nature, the recovery of some imagined Golden Age, a revelation or revolution, a regeneration of humankind's relationship with the sacred world, or any number of recuperative activities.

We open comics studies to Romantic literary history if we keep in mind that many Romantic models persist in the works of succeeding generations. Moore and Williams's place in this diachronic literary history is in how *Promethea* draws on early twentieth-century ideas from the occult, which descend from the French Symbolists, who took up Romantic ideas about one's artistic responsibilities to facilitate human progress through imaginative creativity. This book's larger scope for reading Moore and Williams in context with Romanticism suggests that larger patterns of comics creativity extend from this literary period. Chapters One and Two explore how *Sandman* and *Promethea* contribute to these larger patterns, and they suggest there is a greater Romantic literary history of comics than hitherto suspected. A great way to expand on this idea is to explore the work of artists who are connected to Alan Moore's and Neil Gaiman's work, and in the following chapter, I extend this framework to Mike Carey, Peter Gross, and their series, *The Unwritten*.

Notes

169 William Buckler, *The Victorian Imagination: Essays in Aesthetic Exploration* (New York: New York University, 1980), 37.

170 The concept of *Eyn-Sof* conveys the idea that the Judeo-Christian word and concept of "God" is a human manifestation of a greater divine entity that is beyond human language. Joseph Dan, ed., *The Early Kabbalah*, trans. Ronald Kiener (New York: Paulist Press, 1986), 90.

171 Alan Moore and J. H. Williams III, *Promethea: Book 1* (New York: DC Comics, 2000), 24.

172 Ibid.

173 Tracee Howell, "The Monstrous Alchemy of Alan Moore: *Promethea* as Literacy Narrative," *Studies in the Novel*, 47, no. 3 (2015): 384, doi: 10.1353/sdn.2015.0044 (accessed October 22, 2021).

174 Roderick McGillis, "The Sustaining Paradox: Romanticism and Alan Moore's *Promethea* Novels," in *Time of Beauty, Time of Fear: The Romantic Legacy in the Literature of Childhood*, ed. James Holt McGavran, Jr. (Iowa City: University of Iowa Press, 2012), 200.

175 Howell, 384.

176 McGillis, 205. Douglas Wolk. *Reading Comics: How Graphic Novels Work and What They Mean* (Philadelphia: Da Capo Press, 2007), 245.

177 Alex Romagnoli and Gian Pagnucci, *Enter the Superheroes: American Values, Culture, and the Canon of Superhero Literature* (Lanham, MD: Scarecrow Press, 2013), 96.

178 McGillis, 206.

179 Michael Saler, *As If: Modern Enchantment and the Literary Prehistory of Virtual Reality* (New York: Oxford University Press, 2012), 23.

180 Ibid., 43.

181 Susanna Clark, "The Wonderful Wizard of Northampton: *Watchmen* Writer Alan Moore Talks Sex and Superheroes with Novelist Susanna Clark," *The Telegraph*, last modified October 21, 2019, https://www.telegraph.co.uk/culture/books/authorinterviews/11608804/Susanna-Clark-interviews-Alan-Moore-the-wonderful-wizard-of...-Northampton.html (accessed October 22, 2021).

182 William Blake, *Jerusalem*, in *The Portable Blake*, ed. Alfred Kazin (New York: Penguin Books, 1946), 460.

183 Alan Moore and J. H. Williams III, *Promethea: Book 3* (New York: DC Comics, 2002), 45–47.

184 Ibid., 42

185 McGillis, 204–6.

186 Geoffrey Hartman, "Toward Literary History," *Daedalus*, 99, no. 2 (1970): 364, https://www.jstor.org/stable/20023949 (accessed October 22, 2021).

187 Sale, 10.

188 Charles A. Coulombe, "Hermetic Imagination: The Effect of the Golden Dawn on Fantasy Literature," *Mythlore: A Journal of J. R. R. Tolkien, C. S. Lewis, Charles Williams, and Mythopoeic Literature*, 21, no. 2 (1996): 354.

189 Howell, 382.

190 In its original single-issue print, "The Promethea Puzzle" appears in the final pages of Issue 1, titled "The Radiant Heavenly City."

191 Moore and Williams III, *Promethea: Book 1*, iv.

192 Ibid., v.

193 Howell, 385–86.

194 Ibid., 387.

195 Ibid., 393.

196 Ibid., 384.

197 Moore and Williams III, *Promethea: Book 1*, 129.

198 Jacques Derrida, *Des Tours de Babel*, in *Acts of Religion*, ed. Gil Anidjar, trans. Joseph F. Graham (New York: Routledge, 2002), 131.

199 Ibid., 132.

200 Ibid., 133.

201 Howell, 384.

202 Wolk, 249.

203 Saler, 20.

204 Joshua Landy, "Modern Magic: Jean Eugène Robert-Houdin and Stéphane Mallarmé," in *The Re-Enchantment of the World*, eds. Joshua Landy and Michael Saler (Stanford: Stanford University Press, 2009), 102.

205 Landy and Saler, eds., *The Re-Enchantment of the World* (Stanford: Stanford University Press, 2009), 2.

206 Saler, 3.

207 Ibid., 18–19.

208 Ibid., 19.

209 Ibid., 10.

210 Coulombe, 318.

211 Ibid., 354.

212 See, for instance, W. B. Yeats and Edwin John Ellis's book about William Blake, titled *The Works of William Blake: Poetic, Symbolic, and Critical* (1893).

213 Buckler, 37.

214 Edmund Wilson, *Axel's Castle: A Study of the Imaginative Literature of 1870–1930*, ed. Mary Gordon (New York: Farrar, Straus, and Giroux, 1931), 40.

215 Ibid., 41.

216 Wilson, 12.

217 Ibid., 11.

218 Ibid., 13.

219 Saler, 31.

220 Wilson writes, "Yeats, the ablest of the *fin de siècle* group who tried in London to emulate the French, managed to make Symbolism flourish…Eliot in his earliest poems seems to have been as susceptible to the influence of the Symbolists as to that of the English Elizabethans. Joyce, a master of Naturalism as great as Flaubert, has at the same time succeeded in dramatizing Symbolism by making use of its methods for differentiating between his various characters and their varying states of mind. And Gertrude Stein has carried Mallarmé's principles so far in the directions of that limit where other lungs find air unbreathable as perhaps finally to reduce them to absurdity." From *Axel's Castle*, 21.

221 Wilson, 18.

222 Ibid., 23.

223 Coulombe, 349.

224 Ibid., 350.

225 It is important to distinguish Yeats's ideas about "magic" from the "magic" of popular fantasy worlds, such as J. K. Rowling's wizarding world of *Harry Potter*. Mann explains, "The system of exams in geomancy and alchemy and magical grades may sometimes seem reminiscent of Harry Potter's world, but in the end ritual magic is about aligning the forces of microcosm and macrocosm." The hermetic view is not about physical magic but of raising one's consciousness by aligning the individual to the larger system of the cosmos. Neil Mann, "The Hermetic Order of the Golden Dawn," *The System of Yeats's* A Vision, last Modified October 29, 2006, http://www.yeatsvision.com/GD.html (accessed October 22, 2021).

226 Wilson, 41.

227 W. B. Yeats, quoted in Coulombe, "Hermetic Imagination," 349.

228 Ibid.

229 Alan Moore, quoted in Clark, "The Wonderful Wizard of Northampton."

230 Coulombe, 354.

231 Alan Moore and J. H. Williams III, *Promethea: Book 2* (New York: DC Comics, 2002), 131.

232 Ibid., 135.

233 Ibid., 137.

234 Alan Moore and J. H. Williams III, *Promethea: Book 4* (New York: DC Comics, 2003), 33.

235 Alan Moore and J. H. Williams III, *Promethea: Book 5* (New York: DC Comics, 2005), 182, 187–88.

236 McGillis, 203–4.

237 Lord Byron, "Darkness," in *Lord Byron: Selected Poems*, eds. Susan J. Wolfson and Peter J. Manning (New York: Penguin Books, 1996), 412, lines 69–71.

238 M. H. Abrams, *Natural Supernaturalism: Tradition and Revolution in Romantic Literature* (New York: W. W. Norton & Co., 1971), 334.

239 Ibid.

240 Percy Bysshe Shelley, *Prometheus Unbound: A Lyrical Drama in Four Acts*, in *Romanticism: An Anthology*, ed. Duncan Wu (Malden, MA: Blackwell Publishers, 2012), 1190, Act III, scene iii, lines 47–50.

241 Moore and Williams III, *Promethea: Book 1*, 127–28.

242 Ibid., 127.

243 Moore and Williams III, *Promethea: Book 5*, 53.

244 Ibid., 70.

245 Alan Moore, quoted in Howell, "The Monstrous Alchemy of Alan Moore," 384.

246 Moore and Williams III, *Promethea: Book 3*, 249.

247 Douglas Wolk, *Reading Comics: How Graphic Novels Work and What They Mean* (Philadelphia: Da Capo Press, 2007), 245.

248 Moore and Williams III, *Promethea: Book 3*, 88.

249 Ibid., 96.

250 Moore and Williams III, *Promethea: Book 4,* 111–13.

251 George Khoury, ed., "Chapter III: The Rising," in *The Extraordinary Works of Alan Moore* (Raleigh: TwoMorrows Publishing, 2003), 63.

CHAPTER 3

"And of all these things the Albino whale was the symbol. Wonder ye then at the fiery hunt?" *The Unwritten*, Romantic Organicism, and Paranoia

Placing *The Unwritten*

Isaiah Berlin explains that creative patterns form in spaces/places throughout human history. Such patterns, he suggests, reveal a general way of thinking and a "particular pattern of life."[252] He writes, "The history not only of thought, but of consciousness, opinions, action too, of morals, politics, aesthetics, is…a history of dominant models."[253] Berlin's points are that these models gather energy and persist into later generations, and we can better understand historical moments of creativity if we read these patterns. If we extend these ideas to the mainstream American comic book industry, they suggest that Neil Gaiman, Alan Moore, and their collaborators energized certain aesthetic patterns that persist from the 1980s and into the twenty-first century. These patterns are defined by the ways the artists invent mythologies to highlight their personal ideas about the importance of imagination and creativity, and Mike Carey and Peter Gross's *The Unwritten* is a series that follows these patterns.[254] On one hand, we can firmly ground Carey and Gross's relationship with creative patterns that Gaiman and Moore energized by exploring their direct connections to Gaiman's *Sandman* series. On the other hand, these connections create space to discuss common literary ancestors that Gaiman, Moore and Williams, and Carey and Gross share, and the importance in this reading is at least twofold: It helps us better understand larger patterns of comics creativity, and it also helps us better understand comics' place in larger, historically distinct creative patterns of which traditional literature, film, and other art forms are a part.

The Unwritten first appeared in 2009 as a monthly serialized publication, which was then republished as a twelve-volume set of graphic novels. The first logical step in placing *The Unwritten* in larger patterns of comics creativity is to explore how Carey and Gross's prior work in mainstream comics is directly connected to Gaiman's *Sandman* series. The artists began their tenure in DC Comics's Vertigo division by writing and drawing two *Sandman* spin-off titles: *Books of Magic*[255] and *Lucifer*.[256] These series are defined by their place in a distinct narrative design, and they are helpful for reading *The Unwritten*'s narrative designs. For example, *The Unwritten* and *Books of Magic* follow stories about boy-wizards—named Tommy Taylor and Timothy Hunter respectively—who are destined to become the world's greatest magicians. Throughout *Books of Magic*, Tim interacts with Dream and Death of The Endless, John Constantine, and the Faerie host from William Shakespeare's *A Midsummer Night's Dream*, while the *Lucifer* series continues the story of the biblical figure as he last appears in *Sandman*.[257] On the surface, it is no coincidence that *Books of Magic* and *The Unwritten* are stories about boy-wizards destined to save the world.

What is less clear is that the stories about Lucifer and Timothy Hunter take place in a comic book universe[258] where it is common for new comic book characters to interact with preexisting literary characters, and these narrative dynamics find their way into *The Unwritten*. Comic book universes are typically defined by their porous nature. Stories that seem disconnected may function together as an organic entity or become subsumed by a larger comic book universe. In *The Unwritten*, Carey and Gross take advantage of these dynamics and construct a universe that incorporates all of literary history. *The Unwritten* follows a group of characters—Tom Taylor, Lizzie Hexam, and Richard Savoy—who experience the dissolution of the boundaries between fiction and "reality." Literary characters begin to inhabit the "real world," such as the Creature from Mary Shelley's *Frankenstein*, and Tom, Lizzie, and Savoy gain access to various literary works, including Herman Melville's *Moby-Dick*, C. S. Lewis's *Chronicles of Narnia*, and Lewis Carroll's *Alice's Adventures in Wonderland*. Carey and Gross's process of bringing together new and preexisting characters into one story places *The Unwritten* alongside their earlier work in *Books of Magic* and *Lucifer*, and the importance in reading this creative history suggests that *The Unwritten* is connected to a greater literary history. Like Gaiman's and Moore's designs, Carey and Gross's designs in *The Unwritten* can be traced to Philip José Farmer's Wold Newton stories.[259] This connection opens the series to literary-historical inquiry with twentieth-century fantasy fiction. Like *Sandman*, however, we can take literary-historical perspectives on *The Unwritten* beyond Farmer's narrative designs if we remain open to insights from critical histories outside of comics studies and remain open to ideas about comics' greater literary history.

Literary critical history suggests that we can trace Carey and Gross's creative process to patterns in nineteenth-century European Romanticism. Berlin, for instance, demonstrates that Romantic artists in Germany and England energized the process of making literary history a rich source of mythology,[260] and we find this process in later generations. These ideas suggest that Carey and Gross follow the creative process of Romantic authors, such as William Blake, Percy Bysshe Shelley and their German peers, who use myth to convey "inexpressible vision[s] of the unceasing activity which is life."[261] Here, Berlin captures how Romantic artists understood mythology as a vehicle for conveying ideas about the redemptive roles of artists in larger metaphysical systems. In this way, Romantic myths become a form of personal expression, and myth serves as a vehicle for artists to elevate personal ideas about the redeeming roles of imaginative literature throughout human history. By comparison, Carey and Gross invent a mythology for *The Unwritten* that elevates ideas about the redeeming qualities of imaginative creativity. In the story, imaginative fiction plays a role in freeing humankind from political oppression and tyranny, and artists are responsible for writing "true" stories that reconnect humanity to a larger, organic system. Berlin's framework for reading creative patterns suggests that Carey and Gross use myth in ways that intersect with Romantic antecedents. The artists use myth to dramatize personal ideas about human integrity's dependence on imaginative fiction, and literary criticism offers us new insights into this creative process's ideas about organic systems.

We can better understand Carey and Gross's creative process—and the historical conditions of this process—if we read *The Unwritten* in the context of Romantic ideas about organic systems. For example, Carey and Gross construct *The Unwritten*'s mythology around the figure Leviathan, a metaphysical white whale. We as readers discover that this figure energizes imaginative storytelling from the *Epic of Gilgamesh* up through *Harry Potter*. This figure also symbolizes a greater idea about storytelling. In *The Unwritten: Leviathan* (Volume 4, Issue 23), the title character, Tom Taylor, encounters Leviathan and notices that millions of people form this entity.[262] During this encounter, he describes the figure as symbolizing "the collective unconscious, or something. *The Fictional Unconscious*. The minds of all the millions of people who read my father's books. Or any books."[263] Tom's comments construct Leviathan as a symbol for a living literary psyche. The story's logic is that humankind collectively invests in an organic system of literature, and the imaginative literature for which Leviathan is responsible contains ideas that collectively ensure humankind's freedom and futurity.

Romantic criticism suggests that the historical conditions of *The Unwritten* emerge in the story's drama and its value system for reading creativity. In the story, a secret society, named The Unwritten, hunts Leviathan in an attempt to gain political power and influence. The running logic is that whoever controls the storytelling system can control the way people think and act. In a Romantic framework, Carey and Gross's narrative focus on the redemptive qualities of imagination and creativity becomes a form of personal expression. This reading's importance rests in the ways it establishes Carey and Gross's place in a diachronic literary history of Romanticism alongside Neil Gaiman and Alan Moore. As we see in Chapters One and Two of this book, William Buckler's ideas about "Romantic faith" persisting through nineteenth- and twentieth-century literature can help us better understand artists' Romantic worldviews. For example, Buckler explains that Romantic faith is when an artist measures imaginative creativity's importance to humankind. He goes on to stress three points: early nineteenth-century Romantic artists energized this faith;[264] this faith is expressed in different modes of art;[265] and it "cannot be imaginatively stereotyped."[266] This latter point concedes that many myth-makers in the world think about the roles of imagination and creativity, but they do so in different ways: Romantic faith is as diverse as it is consensual. When we extend these ideas to comics, they suggest that a consensual, Romantic faith in art takes different imaginative forms in *Sandman*, *Promethea*, and *The Unwritten*. In Chapters One and Two, I identify how *Sandman* and *Promethea* become extensions of the Chestertonian and hermetic forms of the imagination, and *The Unwritten* takes on a third form: Romantic organicism. This difference in Romantic faith does not cause problems as much as it strengthens my thesis that Carey and Gross contribute to the patterns that Gaiman and Moore energized in mainstream comics.

In *The Unwritten*, Carey and Gross's Romantic faith highlights the idea that human life shares an organic, symbiotic relationship with a storytelling system. The character Madame Rausch explains, "There is a symbiosis between humanity and Leviathan. We need each other…[I]n the end without story, without the ability to step sideways from fact into hypothesis, human life is untenable."[267] This "symbiosis" is based on ideas about the ways artists develop and maintain an "organic" literary system in order to develop and maintain human integrity. These ideas can be located in a diachronic literary history of Romanticism with some certainty. Charles Armstrong, for example, defines organicism as a dominant model of the Romantic period, and he writes that organicism "is one of [Romanticism's] singularities."[268] What becomes essential in reading Carey and Gross's *The Unwritten* as an extension of organic models is keeping in mind Buckler's ideas that such models persist throughout the twentieth century. Armstrong goes on to trace how many Romantic authors, such as Samuel Taylor Coleridge and Friedrich Schlegel, use organic models to develop ideas about larger biological systems of which all human activity is a part. In these models, artists take on various roles for maintaining humankind's connection to larger, organic systems, and we find these ways of thinking about artists in *The Unwritten*. The importance in reading this narrative dynamic is twofold: It helps us read a greater literary history of comics, and it also contributes to studies in Romanticism. Armstrong asks, "What on earth has happened to organicism? What has become of the vitality and importance of this idea?"[269] *The Unwritten* answers these questions with some authority: We find organicism in comics. Comics help us (re)read literary history. *The Unwritten* becomes part of a larger, historically distinct discourse that extends from Romanticism, and literary-critical history suggests that these discourses provide insight into historical conditions of twenty-first-century creativity.

The Unwritten in Critical Context

The difficulty with reading *The Unwritten* as an extension of Romanticism rests in similar problems we met within *Sandman*'s and *Promethea*'s respective discourses. Prevailing criticism limits Carey and Gross's creative process to postmodern creative practices.[270] Peter Wilkins, for example, describes *The Unwritten* as a "metafictional science fiction" series,[271] and Essi Varis describes the presence of literary characters in *The Unwritten* as "amplif[ying] the pastiche-like quality."[272] These ideas about postmodern metafiction and pastiche suggest that Carey and Gross's creative process is largely defined by the ways that they signal creative influence when their characters interact with preexisting literary elements. Wilkins writes, "*The Unwritten* plays with multiple styles and discourses to show the different levels of its own story as it moves Tom Taylor, the central character, in and out of different diegetic worlds from classic literature."[273] Here, Wilkins reads how the character Tom Taylor gains the ability to inhabit imaginary worlds from different literary works, and his ideas about metafiction suggest that Carey and Gross use these events to inventory literary influences on their creative process. For instance, Carey and Gross connect *The Unwritten* to a greater history of whale literature. The *Leviathan* story arc (Volume 4) is a blatant connection to Thomas Hobbes's *Leviathan*, and Carey and Gross also create a greater network as Tom enters the world of Herman Melville's *Moby-Dick* and sails on the Pequod with the crew. After being swallowed by the whale, Tom meets Rudolf Erich Raspe's Baron Munchausen, the biblical Jonah, Rudyard Kipling's Hibernian Mariner, *Arabian Night*'s Sinbad, and Carlo Collodi's Pinocchio.[274] In Wilkins's framework, Carey and Gross consciously create these interactions to signal the narrative's connections to preexisting literature.

Varis's reading is based on W. G. Müller's concept of "interfigurality," a term that describes a process where "intertextual particles of characters" manifest when characters are self-aware of their own connections to literature.[275] For instance, Carey and Gross encourage readers to understand *The Unwritten*'s connections to Mary Shelley's *Frankenstein*. In the story, Tommy Taylor is a character in a series of fantasy books, who is brought to life in the "real" world by his author-father, Wilson Taylor. Wilson also brings Tommy to life at the Villa Diodati, in Switzerland, where Mary Shelley began writing *Frankenstein*. Moreover, in *Tommy Taylor and the Ship that Sank Twice* (Volume 12), we as readers receive excerpts from Wilson Taylor's journal entries about creating Tom. One reads, "It doesn't matter if all the world thinks I'm a monster, or a mad scientist, or what the hell else."[276] The setting at the Diodati and the character's commentary encourage readers to understand Wilson Taylor's connections to Mary Shelley and Victor Frankenstein. Carey and Gross also develop a relationship between Tom Taylor and Frankenstein's Creature, another character who crosses over into the "real" world. Tom addresses his relationship with the Creature as a being "made by some guy with a God complex."[277] Varis's ideas about interfigurality suggest that these narrative elements encourage readers to understand the story's connections to *Frankenstein* in rather blatant ways. She speculates how such self-aware moments indicate a creative process where Carey and Gross attempt to "[lure] mature readers and [gain] recognition as 'proper' art."[278] In this framework, Varis suggests that the artists intend to elevate comics—a medium typically regarded as lowbrow—through pastiche.

What is missing from *The Unwritten*'s critical discourse is a better understanding of the ways Carey and Gross are self-aware artists who use their story's mythology to establish personal relationships with literary history. *The Unwritten* reimagines literary history as an ongoing growth of imaginative storytelling, and Romantic criticism suggests that this creative process ironically includes Carey and Gross's storytelling. The artists create opportunities for characters to interact with their own literary history, and at the same time, they encourage readers to understand how they consciously "grow" *The Unwritten* from prior stories. This way of reading historical representation in *The Unwritten* suggests that Carey and Gross commit to the story's artistic ideals of participating in the growth of storytelling: *The Unwritten* is an act of Romantic faith. This creative process suggests a greater literary history of the series than the current discourse leads us to believe—one that takes us well before postmodern practices of metafiction and pastiche. Late eighteenth- and early nineteenth-century artists energized ideas about humankind's relationship with larger organic systems.

The importance in reading *The Unwritten* in the context of Romantic organicism strengthens the thesis that a greater Romantic literary history of comics remains unexplored, and remaining open to literary critical insights helps us map comics creativity in the history of emotions.

Building a New Framework: Comics, Literary Criticism, and Romantic Organicism

Ben Saunders calls for comics studies scholars to learn from the critical histories of other fields if the discipline is to survive and thrive.[279] This book puts these ideas into practice and demonstrates what happens when we extend literary-critical ideas to *Sandman*, *Promethea*, and *The Unwritten*. It opens critical conversations to new, historical understandings of comics creativity. Isaiah Berlin's ideas about creative patterns in literary history suggest that reading *The Unwritten*'s connections to Gaiman's *Sandman* and Moore and Williams's *Promethea* highlights larger creative patterns in comics history. In this framework, such patterns reflect ways of thinking and living that are historically distinct, and Romantic patterns become a prevalent characteristic of the mainstream American comic book industry. The importance in this framework is in the way Berlin takes this reading of creative patterns one step further and creates opportunities to explore artistic motives and situate them within larger historical contexts. In this vein, artistic motive allows us to better understand emotional conditions of creativity, and these conditions are far from ahistorical. These ideas suggest that motive becomes legible in *Sandman*, *Promethea*, and *The Unwritten* when we read creative patterns and do two things: First, read narrative forms of Romantic faith as ideas that energize artists' creativity, and second, place each series in a diachronic literary history of Romanticism. Each form of Romantic faith is defined by a historical urgency to create art, and although these forms are distinct from one another, they share common literary ancestors that extend from Romanticism. Chapters One and Two identify how Gaiman and Moore and Williams connect their stories to early twentieth-century forms of Romantic faith that are based on motives for "reenchanting" the world. *The Unwritten* requires us to explore Carey and Gross's faith in context with Romantic motives to reconnect humankind to a larger organic system, and this motive becomes key in locating *The Unwritten* in a larger discourse in the history of emotions.

Studies dedicated to Romantic writers' place in the history of emotions read aesthetic forms and their relevance to an artist's thought and feeling. In these frameworks, an individual's "felt" experience is historically distinct, and the key to placing *The Unwritten* in this history of emotions rests in reading the ways that narrative form becomes an expression of Romantic faith. For instance, Buckler investigates how succeeding generations of Romantic writers commit to ideals about exercising readers' imaginations in "new functional modes,"[280] and he characterizes their creativity as "act[s] of faith."[281] Romantic acts of faith are defined by artists' emotional connections to, and beliefs in, their work's capabilities to set and sustain guidance for human understandings of reality. This understanding of *The Unwritten* posits the ways that the narrative dramatizes Carey and Gross's personal beliefs in, and emotional connections to, their work. Thus, Carey and Gross's creativity differs from Romantic authors only in practice, not in faith or emotional experience. Where poetry served as a primary vehicle for acts of faith in the nineteenth century, Carey and Gross use comics as a vehicle for an act of Romantic faith in the twenty-first century.

In *The Unwritten*, Carey and Gross construct a certain paradigm for thinking about the imagination and creativity as part of larger, organic processes. This paradigm is characterized by ideas about imaginative storytelling's place in an organic system of which all human life and activity are a part, and these aesthetics intersect with well-documented Romantic models that are based on ideas about organic systems. Berlin explains that many Romantic writers believed that "human groups grew in some plant-like or some animal-like fashion, and that organic, botanical and other biological metaphors were more suitable for describing such growth."[282] Armstrong also discusses how Romantic writers, such as Friedrich Schlegel, detail their organic models as a "system of fragments,"[283] and in this model, each part existing in the system is itself an organic whole—a "polyp."[284] The relationship these polyps bear with one another rests on exchanges in the system. All art becomes a larger "system-organism" that is linked to human experiences,[285] and the intersection between Romantic organicism and *The Unwritten* rests in the symbolic value of Leviathan: a living literary psyche that unifies billions of people.

Leviathan is the heart of *The Unwritten*'s mythology, and this entity represents a living, organic system of stories that exists in the minds of the world's readers. The story's rationale posits how artists create imaginary worlds and populate them, and the characters "live" in the minds of readers. The character Lizzie Hexam informs Tom Taylor that as opposed to "for-real-true," fictional characters and imaginary worlds are "story-true."[286] Here, Lizzie's comment suggests an intersection between what is fictional and what is real. People invest in fictional stories and characters *as if* they were real, imagining what fictional characters would do in the everyday situations in which they find themselves. This rationale focuses on the idea that humanity endures because artists participate in an organic process of growing "true" stories, and readers continually respond to and invest in characters as pedagogical models. These characters teach us right from wrong, good from evil, and they ensure human civility and integrity. In short, Leviathan represents a vast, benevolent power of stories, and the Romantic paradigm suggests that Carey and Gross commit to the belief that their story may have these Romantic effects on readers. If we read this organicism in *The Unwritten* as signaling an act of Romantic faith, we create opportunities to make legible Carey and Gross's motives and the emotional conditions of their creativity. In *The Unwritten*, readers have a distinct, organic relationship with the imaginative literature that Leviathan represents, and Carey and Gross's creative process signals the relationship that they hope *The Unwritten* has with their own readers.

An artist's system for reading literary history creates opportunities to explore the artists' intended effects of their work. To this end, Carey and Gross create a myth based on artistic ideals about sustaining an organic system, and the narrative's faith in imaginative literature's capability to reconnect humankind to a larger system reflects Carey and Gross's faith in imaginative literature. This new framework suggests that Carey and Gross commit to artistic ideals about contributing to an organic system that has the capability of connecting millions of people through storytelling. We can take these ideas about organicism one step further by closely examining the ways that this system for reading human history is illusory: It is a personal construct, an imaginary narrative in which art drives human history. It is a fiction, and Romantic criticism suggests that a distinct emotional experience defines the conditions that energize Carey and Gross's creativity: paranoia.

The Unwritten: Romantic Organicism and Historical Conspiracy

In *The Unwritten*, Carey and Gross use myth as a vehicle for reinterpreting human history as an organic system. The mythical figure Leviathan conveys a way of thinking in which all human activity affects and is affected by storytelling, whether personal stories shared among friends, political narratives, or popular fantasy fiction, like *The Lord of the Rings*—and *The Unwritten* itself. This premise suggests that imaginative storytellers act as mediums between a larger organic system and humankind, and when audiences invest in imaginary worlds, their experiences play regenerative, didactic roles in an intellectual, moral vitality.

The importance in reading this value system is in the ways it suggests that Romantic ideas about organic systems endure in twenty-first-century creativity in at least two key ways. First, Carey and Gross's creative process intersects with Romantic authors, like Friedrich Schlegel, who energized ideas about human history being a living "'system-creature' of sorts."[287] Armstrong explains how such interpretive models "attempt to formulate the question of the whole" of human history.[288] This means that many Romantic artists use various aesthetic forms to imagine some kind of organic force or power that unifies humankind and makes it "whole," and in these models, artists become elevated as individuals assuming responsibilities to maintain these powers. When we extend these ideas to *The Unwritten*, they suggest that Carey and Gross formulate the question of the whole by using an aesthetic space to imagine both how history depends on a literary system—Leviathan—and how artists assume responsibilities to liberate humankind.

Second, we can take *The Unwritten*'s narrative ideas about organic systems a step further by reading the ways that Carey and Gross imagine storytelling's connection to humankind's freedom from political oppression and tyranny. This reading suggests that we can make legible Carey and Gross's personal anxieties about human history by reading how they imagine tensions between their craft and historical realities. Armstrong's ideas about organicism, for instance, suggest that Romantic subjects make "no strict separation between poetics and politics…[P]olitical freedom and cultivation of the arts are explicitly linked."[289] This framework suggests that Romantic writers not only imagine but also commit to the creative responsibilities about which they write. In this vein, Carey and Gross use narrative to reimagine human history, and at the same time, they indicate their personal state of historical cognition. This cognitive state produces a historical narrative that imagines how artists defend a system from malevolent forces. Carey and Gross therefore commit to the narrative's artistic ideals about defending human integrity through storytelling, and the importance in reading this dynamic of creative process rests in the ways that aesthetic forms in comics become an extension of Romanticism in the history of emotions.

Prevailing Romantic studies suggest that aesthetic forms dialectically relate to artists' feelings about real world events. This framework suggests that creativity becomes a vehicle for reflecting on historically distinct, "felt" experiences. Thomas Pfau, for instance, reads how Romantic writers express their feelings towards historical events, and he maps a history of nineteenth-century emotional experiences with "early capitalist power structures" and the Napoleonic Wars.[290] Here, Pfau premises his study of Romanticism's place in the history of emotions as an exploration of how aesthetic forms relate to historical states of mind and attitudes toward historical events. Such studies that focus on Romantic myth-making and the persistence of Romantic states of mind are a helpful starting point in reading *The Unwritten*'s formal structures and their relation to Carey and Gross's historical state of mind. Reading these formal structures suggests that *The Unwritten*'s ideas about organicism (Leviathan) and historical conspiracy (The Unwritten) capture a paranoid state of mind. Berlin describes paranoia as one of two "obsessive phenomena which are…very present both in nineteenth- and twentieth-century thought and feeling."[291] Berlin's argument rests on the idea that paranoia and nostalgia are feelings that dominate Romantic literature, and his point is that these creative models persist in creativity.

The Unwritten fits the criteria of Romantic paranoia in the ways that Carey and Gross construct a model for reading human history as a system that artists must defend against larger historical forces. Berlin describes how paranoia manifests in the ways that artists invent artistic images to describe such forces:

> There is a notion that although we individuals seek to liberate ourselves, yet the universe is not to be tamed in this easy fashion. There is something behind, there is something in the depths of the unconscious, or of history; there is something, at any rate, not seized by us which frustrates our dearest wishes. Sometimes it is conceived as a kind of indifferent or even hostile nature, sometimes as the cunning of history…[or] some fearful hostile force lying in wait for us which trips us up when we are on the brink, as we think, of great success.[292]

Here, Berlin describes the ways that paranoid artists invent artistic images that dramatize personal ideas about an urgency to resist historical forces that are always "lying in wait" and ready to "trip us up." *The Unwritten* intersects with this "paranoid" model in the ways Carey and Gross reimagine human history as a system over which two artistic forces compete: historical forces of tyranny and freedom—The Unwritten and Leviathan. In Berlin's framework, Carey and Gross *imagine* something to fear, and this fear becomes personal.

Thomas Pfau takes Berlin's ideas a step further by arguing that Romantic paranoia is a historically distinct "mood" that we can trace across a wide variety of narratives in the nineteenth and twentieth centuries.[293] Pfau creates opportunities to read connections between *The Unwritten* and Romantic paranoia by extending his framework to popular culture. In his study, he observes how Hollywood films are filled with paranoid narratives that update "artifice familiar" with early Romanticism.[294] He writes, "It is worthwhile bearing in mind that popular culture of the past two decades has been filled with conspiratorial narratives…[P]opular cinematic culture of the 1980s and 1990s dramatizes paranoia as a condition experienced by individuals or groups who feel their very status as 'human' to be under siege. From Ridley Scott's *Alien* films to James Cameron's *Terminator* bonanza, from *Blade Runner* to *X-Men* and *The X-Files*."[295] He goes on to stress that such recurring narrative forms "warrant closer attention" in "the media of film and cyberpunk fiction" because they indicate the persistence of Romantic paranoia as a historical state of cognition.[296] What happens when we extend these perspectives to comics is that they suggest a larger discourse of paranoia exists in the medium. *The Unwritten* is a fruitful starting point to extend this paranoia to comics because Carey and Gross imagine that a historical conspiracy takes place, one in which humankind is "under siege" by a secret society with motives to accumulate political power and influence. It is logical to extend Pfau's ideas for reading paranoia to *The Unwritten* if we keep in mind that the heart of the story is a conspiratorial narrative—a paranoid narrative—and this aesthetic form warrants closer attention not only in cyberpunk fiction and popular film but also in comics.

"the only story where the whale wins": *The Unwritten*, Romantic Paranoia, and Melville's *Moby-Dick*

The premise of *The Unwritten* is that a secret society operates behind the scenes of human history. The character Wilson Taylor describes these people as history's "antagonists who never allowed themselves to be named,"[297] hence, they are called The Unwritten. These antagonists employ history's despots and "masters of lies"[298] so that they can maintain political power and influence. They do so by warping stories that exist in the minds of the world's readers—stories that Leviathan represents. Carey and Gross frame The Unwritten's stories as "lies" in the sense that they energize forms of human cruelty, oppression, and tyranny. For instance, in the story, The Unwritten were behind Nazi Germany. In his journal, Wilson Taylor explains that the "Nazis were masters of story, masters of lies; they gave the German Volk a narrative in which they were the heroes, robbed of their greatness by scheming Jews."[299] The logic is that as storytelling drives human history, powerful groups of people attempt to make humankind submit to their lies, to their false narratives—to their own storytelling systems.

Romantic criticism suggests that *The Unwritten* fits the criteria for a paranoid narrative in the ways that Carey and Gross use narrative to rethink human history as a series of "almost successful conspiracies perpetrated against an...'authentic' humanity."[300] In other words, Romantic artists imagine ways humankind's organic unity comes under attack by historical forces of tyranny, and this attack manifests in *The Unwritten* in the form of storytelling. The Unwritten recruit authors to write lies for them, and they ruin authors who write truths. For example, in the issue titled "How the Whale Became" (Issue 5), The Unwritten recruit Rudyard Kipling to "preach the gospel of empire to the nations of Earth,"[301] and his poem "The White Man's Burden" becomes their lie to justify British Imperialism. Issue 5 also highlights how The Unwritten do not like the appeal of Oscar Wilde and the Aesthetic Movement, and they seek to ruin his reputation and any chance for an "enduring appeal," which leads to one of his trials in 1895.[302] Kipling discovers The Unwritten's plot to destroy Wilde's reputation, and he rebels against his employer by writing *The Jungle Books* and *Just So Stories*. In *The Unwritten*, Kipling describes his own stories as "Artless tales in which small and powerless protagonists laid low bigger and more powerful aggressors. I was confident that I had chosen the right weapons to fight my war."[303] Here, Carey and Gross capture the idea that imaginative fiction energizes ideas about human freedom, and Carey and Gross's narrative connections to this literary history suggests that they also establish personal connections to this literary tradition.

Romantic criticism suggests that *The Unwritten*'s narrative ideas about literary history and artistic responsibility rebound on the artists, and these dynamics establish not only Carey and Gross's connections to their own story but also the paranoid conditions of the story. For instance, Pfau explains how paranoid narratives and an artist's personal sense of paranoia are indistinct in Romantic literature. Narrative ideas about artistic responsibility signal creative processes energized by the same "interpretive agitation and urgency"[304] to fulfill artistic responsibility. He writes, "[Paranoia] quickly rebounds on any observer who ventures it as a hypothesis about the formal-aesthetic peculiarities of someone's discourses."[305] Within this framework, narrative ideas about an artistic urgency to defend humanity from malevolent historical forces reflect Carey and Gross's personal sense of artistic urgency to combat those forces. According to Romantic criticism, the importance in such a reading is that it allows us to gauge Carey and Gross's temper when creating *The Unwritten*. This way of reading comics opens up the larger discourse of comics studies to the history of emotions. We can transfer this way of reading narrative across other titles connected to the story—including *Sandman*, *Promethea*, and the larger comic book universes of which these titles are a part. Hence, a larger discursive network of creativity emerges in comics, and the value in such a reading rests in how we can better understand comics creativity as part of a larger cognitive event of which traditional literature, film, and other art forms take part in the unfolding of history.

Against the backdrop of Romanticism, *The Unwritten* suggests that there may be many creative processes in comics that are charged by a cognitive state of paranoia. In the story, the artists *imagine* a hostile force that hijacks authorial power and makes humankind submit to them throughout history, and they *imagine* artistic responsibilities to defend humankind and maintain its connections to a larger, organic system. Romantic criticism asks us to bear in mind that these ways of thinking about human history and artistic responsibility are *illusions*: constructs, fictions, imaginary narratives. Whether artists' historical assessments are accurate does not determine whether their narratives contain paranoid paradigms. The artists use aesthetic spaces to construct versions of reality in which their craft drives human history. Such illusions rebound and provide insight into artists' personal anxieties about their own craft. These anxieties emerge in *The Unwritten* in the narrative ways that Carey and Gross think about the effect of a "text's transferential designs" on its audience.[306] In other words, Romantic artists *imagine* ways that texts affect readers, and narrative ideas about artistic efficacy carry the artists' personal ideas about their work's efficacy. *The Unwritten*'s narrative imperative for artistic ideals therefore becomes Carey and Gross's personal imperative to participate in creative ideals. This personal imperative becomes legible in the narrative ways that Carey and Gross dramatize ideas about truth and lies and focus The Unwritten's hunt for Leviathan. These narrative dynamics strengthen the argument that *The Unwritten* is a paranoid narrative, and this paranoia is magnified in the ways that Carey and Gross sustain narrative connections to Herman Melville's *Moby-Dick* throughout the series. The importance in reading these dynamics is in the ways they contribute to existing conversations about *The Unwritten*'s relationship with Melville's novel and expand the scope of comics scholarship to forms of Romantic paranoia.

The Unwritten's hunt for the white whale is a rather blatant connection to *Moby-Dick*, and Carey and Gross make it a point to capitalize on this aspect of the story in *The Unwritten: Leviathan* (Volume 4). In this arc, Tom and his friends pursue Leviathan to Pittsfield, Massachusetts, where Herman Melville wrote the novel, and it is here where prevailing criticism begins to explore *The Unwritten*'s connections to *Moby-Dick*. Peter Wilkins's work, for instance, investigates Carey and Gross's connections to Melville's creative process, as he determines *The Unwritten*'s fidelity to *Moby-Dick* in two ways: First, he comparatively reads how Carey and Gross connect *The Unwritten* to preexisting whale literature in ways consistent with how Melville connects the novel to a larger mythology of sea creatures. He writes, "*The Unwritten* stays true to the novel's intertextual web by weaving itself into the network of whale literature into which Melville wove *Moby-Dick*."[307] Second, Wilkins explores *The Unwritten*'s narrative fidelity to *Moby-Dick* when Tom Taylor gains entrance to the seafaring world of the novel and assumes a role on the Pequod. Tom plays Bulkington, and Ahab takes on the appearance of Wilson Taylor. Wilkins concludes that "[b]oth character transcriptions display a keen understanding of the novel. Authorial power is exactly what Ahab demands, and the curious uncertainty of Bulkington's status in the text fits Tom's unstable position in *The Unwritten*: he might disappear at any time."[308] Critical opportunities arise with these comments that suggest Wilson Taylor seeks authorial power in ways that Ahab uses authorial power. What we can add to Wilkins's ideas are the ways Carey and Gross sustain connections between *Moby-Dick* and *The Unwritten* throughout the twelve volumes, not just the *Leviathan* arc. Moreover, they "weave" *The Unwritten* not only into a larger mythology of sea creatures but also into a larger system for reading literature: organicism. These larger contexts of Carey and Gross's creative process suggest that another set of characters suited for comparative study with Ahab and Moby Dick are The Unwritten and Leviathan.

We can take Wilkins's ideas a step further by reading how Carey and Gross maintain fidelity not only to Melville's characters but also his paranoia. This critical step helps strengthen the hypothesis that Carey and Gross's creative processes fit the criteria of Romantic paranoia. Berlin, for instance, describes how paranoia manifests in the ways that nineteenth-century writers construct "great images dominating humankind," and these images "spread into every sphere of human activity" in the nineteenth century.[309] Many Romantic authors committed to beliefs that such images could convey otherwise ineffable truths about life, the universe, and one's state of being, and one such image is Moby Dick. In "The Whiteness of the Whale," Melville's character Ishmael describes the mythic proportions of the figure:

> Aside from those more obvious considerations touching Moby-Dick, which could not but occasionally awaken in any man's soul some alarm, there was another thought, or rather vague, nameless horror concerning him, which at times by its intensity completely overpowered all the rest, and yet so mystical and well nigh ineffable was it, that I almost despair of putting it in a comprehensible form. It was the whiteness of the whale that above all things appalled me…
>
> [I]t is at once the most meaning symbol of spiritual things, nay, the very veil of the Christian's Deity; and yet should be as it is, the intensifying agent in things the most appalling to mankind…And of all these things the Albino whale was the symbol. Wonder ye then at the fiery hunt?[310]

Melville's Moby Dick represents some greater power of nature that is sacred, holy, sublime, and inscrutable. It is some ineffable force of which human life is at the mercy, and Carey and Gross directly connect the mythical image of Leviathan to this figure. An important distinction is that Leviathan represents an organic force of storytelling that affects all human life, whereas Moby Dick represents some force of nature itself. These differences do not cause problems as much as strengthen the argument that Carey and Gross's creative process intersects with Melville's process. Wilkins describes *Moby-Dick* as inviting "transformative engagement...In place of the 'don't touch me' aura of the 'masterpiece,' *Moby-Dick* says 'play with me.'"[311] On one hand, this transformative "play" between Moby Dick and Leviathan occurs in the ways that Leviathan takes on the meaning of storytelling's power over human unity, and on the other hand, this play also occurs between Melville's Ahab and Carey and Gross's The Unwritten.

Carey and Gross transform Ahab's hunt for Moby Dick into The Unwritten's hunt for Leviathan, and this narrative consistency creates opportunities to explore how Melville's paranoia orders and designs *The Unwritten*'s larger paranoid narrative. Wilkins suggests that "authorial power is exactly what Ahab demands," and he continues to describe how Wilson Taylor assumes a tyrannical role in the story that is akin to Ahab.[312] In *Moby-Dick*, Ahab represents the dangers of despots and authorial power. He demands that the crew submit to his absolute faith in his mission, and this faith leads to the crew's destruction. Wilkins's concerns, however, mainly rest in *The Unwritten*'s fidelity to *Moby-Dick* at the narrative level in one volume of the series (*Leviathan*), whereas Carey and Gross sustain connections to Melville's creative process throughout the twelve volumes. *The Unwritten*'s larger narrative suggests that The Unwritten bend humankind to their will and hunt Leviathan just as Ahab bends the crew to his will and hunts Moby Dick. Like Ahab, the cabal represents the dangers of despots and authorial power. Moreover, Carey and Gross explicitly connect The Unwritten to Ahab when a character named Mister Pullman wounds Leviathan by stabbing Tom. During this scene, quotes from *Moby-Dick* appear in the background that read, "There is a wisdom that is woe; but there is a woe that is madness...From hell's heart I stab at thee."[313] Throughout the rest of the narrative, Tom and his friends must learn how to heal Leviathan and prevent The Unwritten's goal of global domination. This tension between The Unwritten and Leviathan intersects with Melville's Romantic paranoia in the narrative anxiety about despots and control of the written word.

Romantic criticism helps us read and better understand not only how *The Unwritten*'s narrative paranoia is an extension of *Moby-Dick* but also how paranoia becomes a condition of Melville's and Carey and Gross's creativity. Pfau describes how paranoia becomes embedded in narratives where artists *imagine* hostile historical situations and *imagine* ways of resisting them: "the romantic individual appears both engulfed within a volatile historical situation *and* struggling to defend against [it]."[314] These ideas suggest that Romantic paranoia manifests in *The Unwritten* in the ways Carey and Gross *imagine* human history as a system over which two forces compete: the powers of truth and lies. In the story, Leviathan and The Unwritten are always in an unstable production of meaning, always in an unstable production of truth and lies, and artists who write imaginative fiction become champions of truth throughout history. Romantic criticism suggests that the narrative's historical urgency to communicate truths through imaginative fiction confirm Carey and Gross's personal ideas about the historical urgency to communicate truths through their imaginative fiction, *The Unwritten*. The importance in recognizing these artistic ideals at the narrative level rests in how the ideals make legible the paranoid conditions energizing the artists' creativity on personal levels. These conditions become legible when Carey and Gross finish the story and, at the same time, confirm their role in contributing to Leviathan's growth—participating in a paranoid historical narrative.

In the last chapter of *The Unwritten: Apocalypse* (Volume 11), Tom Taylor defeats his enemies by pulling them into "the only story where the whale wins"—*Moby-Dick*.[315] Tom sacrifices himself in using the Pequod as bait to lure Moby Dick and allows the whale to consume him and the last of The Unwritten—Mister Pullman and Madame Rausch. Tom fulfills his heroic purpose, and the event marks the end of the narrative: Carey and Gross have finished the story. Pfau's framework for reading paranoia suggests how in completing *The Unwritten*, Carey and Gross reconfirm their commitment to an illusory artistic ideal: Carey and Gross's reality remains unchanged despite their ideas about imaginative fiction's efficacy. Thus, literary-critical history also suggests that nineteenth-century Romantic paranoia not only persists into, but remains formally unchanged in, the larger public discourse of mainstream comic books.

Like Neil Gaiman and Alan Moore and J. H. Williams III, Carey and Gross suggest that they inherit responsibilities to participate in an ongoing production of art, and my point is that this body of work in mainstream comics forms an aesthetic pattern that allows us to gauge the temper of historical moments. Carey and Gross, Gaiman, and Moore and Williams recall Romantic values of imaginative creativity, artistic identity, and responsibility. These ideals become fundamental parts of narrative structure and impetus in *The Unwritten*, *Sandman*, and *Promethea*. My framework suggests that this Romantic faith is charged by the artists' anxieties about their own historical situations. *The Unwritten* reveals that historical conspiracy is a paranoid paradigm that has been formally unchanged since the Romantic period. We find a greater number of comic book artists giving pride of place to understandings of art that recall Romantic faith and paranoia, and these dynamics are largely unexplored in critical discourse. One tendency of literary scholarship is to recognize bodies of work with thematic and aesthetic similarities, and the Romantic literary history of *The Unwritten*, *Promethea*, and *Sandman* suggests that we can place comics in the history of emotions. Moreover, this argument suggests that we can trace paranoia across a variety of writings connected to *Sandman*, *Promethea*, and *The Unwritten*, and these connections indicate that comics are part of a larger, cognitive event in the unfolding of history. The final chapter of this book uses this framework to explore how comics help us better understand that paranoia is a fundamental state of nineteenth-, twentieth-, and twenty-first-century historical experience.

Notes

252 Isaiah Berlin, *The Roots of Romanticism* (Princeton: Princeton University Press, 1999), 2.

253 Ibid.

254 It is worth noting that *Sandman*, *Promethea*, and *The Unwritten* are all published by DC Comics, but each title debuted under different imprints. For instance, Alan Moore and J. H. Williams III's *Promethea* was first published under the label America's Best Comics (ABC), which was an imprint of Jim Lee's WildStorm. DC later absorbed the company and, in 1999, shut it down and republished the series under their Vertigo moniker. *Sandman* first debuted under DC Comics but was later published as a Vertigo title, and *The Unwritten* debuted under the Vertigo moniker. Later, in 2019, DC shut down the Vertigo imprint and is currently publishing all three titles under the new Black Label imprint.

255 Gross first wrote and contributed artwork to *The Books of Magic* from 1994 until 2000. From 1994 until 1998, he contributed artwork to the series, and he then took over writing *and* drawing the title until 2000, ending his run with Issue 75.

256 Carey's work on *Lucifer* debuted in June 2000, and Gross later joined the series's creative team in Issue 5. Carey and Gross collaborated on the *Lucifer* title until August 2006.

257 Lucifer Morningstar is a wingless angel who owns a piano bar on Earth after abandoning his responsibilities in Hell.

258 Please refer to the Conclusion of this book for a longer discussion about comic book universes. In it, I discuss how a comic book universe is defined by "teams of artists who simultaneously tell stories about individual characters existing in the same imaginary space/place but appearing across different publication titles...Each character's actions—whether in a solo title, a crossover event, or team narrative—can affect the entire comics universe."

259 A longer discussion of Neil Gaiman's and Alan Moore's connections to Farmer's Wold Newton Universe can be found in Chapter One of this book.

260 Berlin, 122.

261 Ibid.

262 Mike Carey and Peter Gross, *The Unwritten: Leviathan* (New York: DC Comics, 2011), 111.

263 Ibid.

264 "[A] sacred pungency had been created by Blake, Wordsworth, Keats, Shelley, and by the flow of Germany that was released into England by Coleridge and, in a more strictly literary fashion, by Carlyle." William Buckler, *The Victorian Imagination: Essays in Aesthetic Exploration* (New York: New York University, 1980), 4.

265 "[A] difference of practice and the motive for practice." Ibid., 38.

266 Ibid., 58.

267 Mike Carey and Peter Gross, *The Unwritten: The Wound* (New York: DC Comics, 2013), 48.

268 Charles Armstrong, *Romantic Organicism: From Idealist Origins to Ambivalent Afterlife* (New York: Palgrave MacMillan, 2003), 5.

269 Ibid., 1.

270 Please see the Introduction of this book for a longer discussion of how prevailing criticism tends to limit understandings of all three series to postmodern ideas. Such limitations seem to be a symptom of a larger issue in comics studies.

271 Peter Wilkins, "An Incomplete Project: Graphic Adaptations of *Moby-Dick* and the Ethics of Response," in *Transforming Anthony Trollope: Dispossession, Victorianism and Nineteenth-Century Word and Image*, ed. Simon Grennan and Laurence Grove (Belgium: Leuven University Press, 2015), 225.

272 Essi Varis, "Something Borrowed: Interfigural Characterization in Anglo-American Fantasy Comics," in *Framescapes: Graphic Narrative Intertexts*, ed. Mikhail Peppas and Sanabelle Ebrahim (Oxford: Inter-Disciplinary Press, 2016), 3.

273 Wilkins, 225.

274 See Mike Carey and Peter Gross, *The Unwritten: Leviathan* (New York: DC Comics, 2011), 92.

275 Varis, 4.

276 Mike Carey and Peter Gross, *The Unwritten: Tommy Taylor and the Ship that Sank Twice* (New York: DC Comics, 2014), 113.

277 Mike Carey and Peter Gross, *The Unwritten: On to Genesis* (New York: DC Comics, 2012), 126.

278 Varis, 3.

279 Please see the Introduction of this project for a discussion of Saunders in context with the larger discourse of comics studies. Ben Saunders, "Divisions in Comics Scholarship," *PMLA*, 124, no. 1 (2009): 292–93, www.jstor.org/stable/25614270 (accessed October 22, 2021).

280 Buckler, 38.

281 Ibid., 37.

282 Berlin, 61.

283 Friedrich Schlegel, in Charles Armstrong's *Romantic Organicism*, 44.

284 Ibid., 40.

285 Ibid., 43.

286 Carey and Gross, *The Unwritten: Leviathan*, 28.

287 Friedrich Schlegel, in Charles Armstrong's *Romantic Organicism*, 15.

288 Ibid., 13.

289 Ibid., 40.

290 He writes, "[F]irst by the divisive impact of the French Revolution, next by...postrevolutionary warfare, and finally by a post-Napoleonic European Restoration." Thomas Pfau, *Romantic Moods: Paranoia, Trauma, and Melancholy, 1790–1840* (Baltimore: Johns Hopkins University Press, 2005), 1.

291 Berlin, 106.

292 Ibid., 106–7.

293 Pfau, 2.

294 Ibid., 83.

295 Ibid., 82.

296 Ibid.

297 Mike Carey and Peter Gross, *The Unwritten: Tommy Taylor and the Bogus Identity* (New York: DC Comics, 2010), 128.

298 Ibid.

299 Ibid.

300 Pfau, 83-84.

301 Mike Carey and Peter Gross, *The Unwritten: Tommy Taylor and the Bogus Identity* (New York: DC Comics, 2010), 113.

302 Ibid., 111–12.

303 Ibid., 122.

304 Pfau, 81.

305 Ibid., 79.

306 Ibid., 91.

307 Wilkins, 226.

308 Ibid., 225–26.

309 Berlin, 124.

310 Herman Melville, *Moby-Dick; or, The Whale* (New York: W. W. Norton & Co., 2018), 151, 156–57.

311 Wilkins, 225.

312 Ibid.

313 Mike Carey and Peter Gross, *The Unwritten: Tommy Taylor and the War of Words* (New York: DC Comics, 2012), 201, 203.

314 Pfau, 81.

315 Mike Carey and Peter Gross, *The Unwritten: Apocalypse* (New York: DC Comics, 2014), 161.

MOOD
IN
COMICS

CONCLUSION

Mood in Comics

Scholars' concerns with classifying comics as a literary medium tend to focus on comics' image-text nature and the question of whether "comics possess the kinds of values that are especially important in great literature."[316] These concerns motivate some comic book scholars[317] to move beyond generic distinctions and examine the ways that artists use image and text to create narrative structures, including characterization, plot, theme, and artistic purpose. In this vein, some narrative conventions of comics descend from literature, and we can trace them to existing literary paradigms. Such ideas energized this book's exploration of historical representation and personal expression in Neil Gaiman's *Sandman*, Alan Moore and J. H. Williams III's *Promethea*, and Mike Carey and Peter Gross's *The Unwritten*. I read the artists' creative process of reimagining literary history with invented mythologies, and then placed these processes in a diachronic literary history of Romanticism.

The value in reading comics in terms of Romanticism is that it leads to larger conversations we could (and should) be having about historical representation, literary history, and comparative study. The problems with existing studies are not so much in the ways scholars comparatively explore comics nor in the ways scholars stress the importance of reading historical representation in nonfiction comics.[318] These studies, in fact, create important foundations for scholarly inquiry. The problem is that critical narratives tend to be limited to particular literary histories and genres, and my book has shown, with some certainty, that we can open up conversations about a broader literary history and a broader portrayal of historical experience in comics, especially in mainstream fiction.[319] The boundaries between fiction and nonfiction are not as static as critical narratives tend to treat them, and certain narrative structures and creative processes need to be understood in different literary-historical contexts. Each chapter of this book uses these premises to focus on the ways that Gaiman, Moore and Williams, and Carey and Gross invent mythologies that highlight ideas about art's redeeming functions in human history, and each chapter argues that such historical representations intersect with personal creative processes that we find in nineteenth-century European Romanticism. Extending nineteenth- and twentieth-century literary critical history to comics and exploring the artists' creative processes leads to larger discourses of which traditional literature, film, and other art forms are a part.

Gaiman's, Moore and Williams's, and Carey and Gross's ways of thinking about art can be placed in a diachronic literary history of Romanticism, and each study in this book reveals that there is still a plenitude to explore. I explore *Sandman* and *Promethea* in terms of the larger cultural project to "reenchant modernity,"[320] and then I take this framework one step further in Chapter Three, where I examine *The Unwritten* and uncover a larger pattern of Romantic faith[321] in mainstream comics creativity. I conclude Chapter Three by discussing how this faith creates what is otherwise known as a "mood." Romantic studies suggest that mood is far from ahistorical,[322] and when we extend these ideas to comics, they suggest that the creative processes in *Sandman*, *Promethea*, and *The Unwritten* are all energized by a certain mood energized in the Romantic period: paranoia. The value in this framework is in the ways that it helps us read a greater spectrum of historical representation in comics, beyond traumatic experiences and "vicious historical realities,"[323] and it helps us read the ways that mainstream comics are part of an ongoing current of paranoia that has defined the larger public discourse of Western culture since the Romantic period.

For example, Thomas Pfau's framework for reading mood suggests that Romantic paranoia emerges where artists use aesthetic spaces to *imagine* historical forces (e.g., political, economic, or technological) against which humanity must fight. On one hand, the Romantics are notorious for creating narratives in which they express personal faith in the power of art to combat such forces. On the other, they use narrative in self-reflective ways to explore personal beliefs about their own craft and its importance to humankind. Pfau's framework is useful in reading how Romantic paranoia also emerges in comics where artists *imagine* the urgency to create art and combat hostile historical forces. We find this sense of artistic urgency in *Sandman*, *Promethea*, and *The Unwritten*. These artists use narrative to imagine and evaluate historical forces, and they posit how historical resolutions can be achieved by aesthetic means. In this way, the artists' Romantic faith in creativity signals the artists' Romantic paranoia.

Paranoia emerges as a consensus in *Sandman*, *Promethea*, and *The Unwritten* in at least two ways: At the narrative level, the artists promote ideas about the redeeming qualities of art in the fight against historical forces, and on another level, their creative processes are self-reflective. In *Sandman*, for example, literature fulfills some psychical need for humankind as it confronts modernity, and the title character, Morpheus, obsesses over his responsibilities to maintain the human psyche. In *Promethea*, too, Moore and Williams imagine a future desacralized by technology and "meaningless" art, and the narrative encourages readers to understand why stories like *Promethea* are necessary to maintain humankind's connections to the sacred. In *The Unwritten*, Carey and Gross construct ideas about the urgency to engage imaginative creativity in an effort to fight forces of tyranny and oppression. Each creative process is defined by the ways the artists create stories *about the importance of creating stories*. They are self-reflective, and therefore, the artists commit to the artistic ideals that they invent.[324] Pfau's framework suggests that these artistic ideals are inherently paranoid ideals. The stories become tools for the artists to negotiate personal historical experiences and commit to personal artistic ideals; they imagine a world in which their craft becomes a driving force of human history and integrity. However idealistic or correct their concept of history is made to be, Romantic studies encourage us to remember that an artist's ideas about history are "constructs, fictions, and imaginary narratives."[325] The artists' sense of urgency to create art and fulfill some ideal is an *imaginary* and, thus, paranoid narrative.

Patterns of creativity make legible ways of thinking and living that a culture obeys, and *Sandman*, *Promethea*, and *The Unwritten* form a pattern that makes paranoia legible in mainstream comics. My conclusions challenge prevailing ideas about fiction and nonfiction by suggesting that mainstream fiction, too, is a place where comic book artists negotiate complex historical experiences. We are, then, left with at least one question: What happens when we can trace this creative pattern—this paranoia—across larger comic book universes? What happens when Gaiman's personal ideas about storytelling are attached to his characters that appear in titles outside of *Sandman*? Similarly, what happens when the character Promethea meets characters outside of *Promethea*? What happens when characters in *The Unwritten* cross over into Bill Willingham's popular series *Fables*? Two convincing answers are that we chart paranoia across a broad spectrum of comics creativity, and we historicize paranoia as an essential psychological condition in the nineteenth, twentieth, and twenty-first centuries.

Paranoia: A Discursive Profile of Comic Book Universes

The concept of Romantic paranoia offers a way to understand thought and feeling at work in *Sandman*, *Promethea,* and *The Unwritten*, and it makes the bridge from Romanticism to comics studies a fairly easy task. Not only can we trace paranoia from the Romantic period and into popular culture, but we can also trace this paranoia into comic book adaptations in popular films.[326] The importance of extending this framework to comic books rests in how it suggests a greater number of comics are part of a larger, historically distinct psychological profile. Paranoia becomes part of the psychological profile of the nineteenth, twentieth, and twenty-first centuries in the ways that people create and invest in narratives that *imagine* humankind under siege and *imagine* ways of defending humankind. Whether their historical assessments are accurate does not determine whether the narratives contain paranoid paradigms. The artists' "symbolic representation" is defined by "a volatile historical situation *and* struggling to defend against…modernity."[327] These ideas suggest that Gaiman, Moore and Williams, and Carey and Gross construct paranoid narratives that convey a perception of history in which artists must defend humankind against hostile forces. Thus, comics make paranoia legible in our culture's discursive profile, and we can complement these ideas with prevailing studies in comics to help create a more convincing case. We can explore how paranoia becomes a formal structure of the larger comic book universes of which *Sandman*, *Promethea*, and *The Unwritten* are a part.

Cyril Camus's ideas about Gaiman and Moore's personal and professional connections are a useful starting point for reading paranoia on a greater scale in comics creativity. On one hand, Camus explores how Moore and Gaiman energized a distinctive "mood" in comics creativity in the 1980s and early 1990s, but he never identifies this mood beyond "dark fantasy."[328] He concludes that exploring Moore's and Gaiman's creative processes are "likely to illuminate many aspects of contemporary popular fiction."[329] If we combine Camus's ideas with Pfau's framework, the result suggests that Gaiman and Moore's "mood"—their paranoia—is embedded in some of mainstream comics' most characteristic titles. Pfau suggests that one way of "gauging the temper of a particular period…is to identify a dominant rhetorical or formal-aesthetic pattern,"[330] and we can reveal paranoia in the larger discourse of mainstream comic books if we trace *Sandman*'s, *Promethea*'s, and *The Unwritten*'s connections to other titles in their respective comic book universes. These ideas suggest that tracing these relationships is likely to illuminate paranoia as an integral part of mainstream fiction, in general.

A comic book universe is defined by teams of artists who simultaneously tell stories about individual characters who appear across different publication titles but who exist in the same imaginary space/place. The exceptions to individual characters appearing in solo titles are crossover events (when the events and characters of one title affect or are affected by the events of another title) and team narratives (when characters from multiple titles all appear in one title, e.g., *The Justice League*). Each character's actions—whether in a solo title, a crossover event, or team narrative—can affect the entire comic book universe. For example, *Sandman* is a solo title, but the events in *Sandman* take place in the DC Universe (DCU), where Superman, Batman, and Wonder Woman exist. The first way that Gaiman attaches the narrative to this universe is in "Imperfect Hosts" (Issue 2 of the series), wherein the houses of Secrets and Mysteries appear.[331] Not only has DC Comics owned the rights to the *House of Mystery* and *House of Secrets* horror comics since the 1950s, but DC owns the rights to incorporate the houses of Secrets and Mystery as imaginary spaces/places within their stories. They are spaces/places beyond "reality" that appear in multiple DC titles, including: *Sandman*, Alan Moore and John Totleben's *Saga of the Swamp Thing*, Jamie DeLano's *Hellblazer*, and Peter Milligan's *Justice League Dark*. Furthermore, characters and events in *Sandman* affect the entire DCU, and we see this influence as recently as Dream's interactions with Batman and Superman in the 2017 comic book series *Dark Nights: Metal*. In this title, all storytelling is the property of Dream, and he loses control of the stories that are told, which affects the entire DC Universe: The heroes must prevent an apocalyptic event by discovering truths about the "Dark Multiverse" through the power of stories—through the power of Dream, the Prince of Stories. This event helped shape the future of the DCU at the time of its publication, and it simultaneously launched four titles in what is currently known as the *Sandman* Universe. What matters for our purposes is that a large body of work emerges from *Sandman*, and with it, a larger pattern emerges in the DCU—one that maintains Gaiman's ideas about the ways stories set and sustain guidance for human understandings of reality. The larger comic book universe often promotes the idea that artists must protect humanity by telling stories that maintain "shadow-truths" about the world. In this way, Gaiman's value system for reading human history in *Sandman* often becomes a formal structure of the larger DCU, and this value system is defined by Romantic paranoia. We can verify Gaiman's "paranoia" across the comic book universe.

In a similar way, Carey and Gross's *The Unwritten* is a title published by DC Comics, but it is not directly attached to the DCU. However, Carey and Gross conduct a crossover event with another DC Comics title, Bill Willingham's *Fables*. In *The Unwritten*, Tom Taylor moves through imaginary worlds, and he enters Willingham's Fabletown. Fabletown is an imaginary community that contains characters from traditional fairy tales, folklore, and legend, such as Snow White, the Big Bad Wolf, and, among others, Prince Charming. The crossover event not only connects *The Unwritten* to a larger discourse, but it also promotes Carey and Gross's ideas about larger systems of storytelling. In the event, the character Frau Totenkinder's commentary encourages readers to understand how stakes in the real world depend on the stakes in imaginative worlds—that the real world is shaped by storytelling. She says, "I have *read* your story, and seen my own reflection there…All worlds begin somewhere. And end somewhere." Tom Taylor responds, "But then—then my world would be inside Leviathan [a story system]. It would *all* be."[332] Here, the subtext encourages readers to understand that the real world—and our understandings of it—reflects stories; the integrity of human experience is directly linked to the stories we tell ourselves to understand the world and our place in it. It is an organic, symbiotic relationship. This crossover event promotes Carey and Gross's personal ideas about storytelling as an organic system linked to human integrity, and Pfau's framework suggests that the artists' Romantic faith in storytelling indicates both series' paranoid formal structures.

Likewise, Moore and Williams's *Promethea* is set in the same comic book universe as *Tom Strong*, another America's Best Comics title Moore wrote with artist Chris Sprouse at the time. In Issue 36 of *Tom Strong* (the final issue), Promethea energizes an apocalypse of the human imagination to reconnect humankind with divine energies. The character Tom Strong addresses it as "the ultimate human moment."[333] Just as the events in *Promethea* affect the characters in *Tom Strong*, Moore and Williams's ideas about the need for imaginative creativity in *Promethea* affect the formal structure of *Tom Strong*. In the final issue, Moore and Sprouse connect with Moore and Williams's ideas about the human imagination and the ways that artists must awaken humankind to "new details, new layers of meaning" in the world.[334] *Promethea*'s ideas about art and artistic responsibility become formal structures of *Tom Strong*, and Pfau's framework suggests that paranoia is a formal principle organizing both narratives.

Tracing paranoia across the larger comic book universes of which *Sandman*, *Promethea*, and *The Unwritten* are a part charts a vast network of paranoid creativity. If we remain open to insights from critical histories outside of comics studies, we create opportunities to read not only comic book creativity but also ourselves as part of a larger history extending from the nineteenth century. Romantic studies offer comics ways of exploring the medium as part of a historically distinct cognitive event, and these studies suggest that paranoia is a historical condition of comics creativity. If we extend this paradigm further into popular culture, it is likely to illuminate mood as a historical condition of creativity in other titles, mediums, and creators. Much work is yet to be done, especially with the ways comics have come to dominate many forms of media. Pfau writes, "Emotions thus are not 'owned' by an individual…but, instead, are experienced as a [historical] dynamic or mood,"[335] and these ideas suggest that the emotions comic book artists express are part of historically distinct networks. We can start to bring these networks to light by reading Romantic paranoia in popular comic book universes. *Sandman*, *Promethea*, and *The Unwritten* contain paranoia as a dominant formal-aesthetic paradigm, and tracing this paradigm across mainstream fiction reveals an emotion that dominates Western culture. We can further develop this line of historical inquiry for the larger discourse of comics studies if we accept mood as a formal-aesthetic paradigm and if we remain open to critical histories outside of comics. We need to have a larger, more inclusive conversation about literary history and mood in comics to have a better understanding of historical moments of creativity. Mood warrants closer attention in comics studies as an integral part of the medium's formal structures. We must consider this dynamic to achieve more comprehensive scholarly inquiries of genre, creative process, and contemporary fiction.

Notes

316 Aaron Meskin, "Comics as Literature?" *British Journal of Aesthetics*, 49, no. 3 (2009): 220, doi:10.1093/aesthj/ayp025 (accessed October 22, 2021).

317 Ibid., 224.

318 Please see the Introduction to this book for a larger discussion of how prevailing criticism tends to privilege nonfiction and limit comparative readings to superhero fiction and classical and religious texts. See, for instance, Hillary Chute's "Comics as Literature?" and George Kovacs and C. W. Marshall's *Classics and Comics*. Hillary Chute, "Comics as Literature? Reading Graphic Narrative," *PMLA*, 123, no. 2 (2008): 452, https://www.jstor.org/stable/25501865 (accessed October 22, 2021); George Kovacs and C. W. Marshall, *Classics and Comics* (New York: Oxford University Press, 2011).

319 Please see the Introduction for a discussion of the deep-seated biases against mass culture media and the American comic book industry.

320 Michael Saler, *As If: Modern Enchantment and the Literary Prehistory of Virtual Reality* (New York: Oxford University Press, 2012), 19.

321 I use William Buckler's ideas about Romantic "faith" to explore *Sandman*, *Promethea*, and *The Unwritten* throughout much of the book. William Buckler, *The Victorian Imagination: Essays in Aesthetic Exploration* (New York: New York University, 1980), 37.

322 Thomas Pfau, *Romantic Moods: Paranoia, Trauma, and Melancholy, 1790–1840* (Baltimore: Johns Hopkins University Press, 2005), 81.

323 Hillary Chute, "Comics as Literature? Reading Graphic Narrative," *PMLA*, 123, no. 2 (2008): 457, https://www.jstor.org/stable/25501865 (accessed October 18, 2021).

324 Please see Chapters One through Three for details about the artists' commitments to artistic ideals.

325 Pfau, 79.

326 Pfau, for instance, writes, "From Ridley Scott's *Alien* films to James Cameron's *The Terminator* bonanza, from *Blade Runner* to *X-Men* and *The X-Files*...conspiracies shrewdly conceived and robotically executed by the abstract forces of global capital ultimately target for elimination the very idea of our 'essential' humanity." This framework provides both a timeframe in which this paranoia is prevalent in creativity (the 1980s and '90s) and a link to comic book source texts (Marvel's *X-Men*). Ibid., 81.

327 Ibid.

328 Cyril Camus, "Neil Gaiman: A Portrait of the Artist as a Disciple of Alan Moore," *Studies in Comics*, 2, no. 1 (2011): 156, doi:10.1386/stic.2.1.147_1 (accessed October 22, 2021).

329 Ibid.

330 Pfau, 77.

331 Neil Gaiman, *Sandman: Preludes & Nocturnes* (New York: DC Comics, 1988), 64.

332 Mike Carey, Peter Gross, and Bill Willingham, *The Unwritten Fables* (New York: DC Comics, 2014), 123.

333 Alan Moore and Chris Sprouse, *Tom Strong* (La Jolla: America's Best Comics, 2006), 8.

334 Ibid., 12.

335 Pfau, 31.

BIBLIOGRAPHY

BIBLIOGRAPHY

Abrams, M. H. *Natural Supernaturalism: Tradition and Revolution in Romantic Literature*. New York: W. W. Norton & Co., 1971.

Armstrong, Charles. *Romantic Organicism: From Idealist Origins to Ambivalent Afterlife*. New York: Palgrave MacMillan, 2003.

Berlatsky, Noah. "Superhero Stories Aren't Myths. They're Anti-Myths." *Pacific Standard* (April 23, 2018). https://psmag.com/social-justice/superhero-stories-arent-myths-theyre-anti-myths (accessed October 18, 2021).

Berlin, Isaiah. *The Roots of Romanticism*. Princeton: Princeton University Press, 1999.

Blake, William. "Jerusalem." In *The Portable Blake*, 445–93. Edited by Alfred Kazin. New York: Penguin Books, 1946.

Bratman, David. "A Game of You—Yes, *You*." In *The Sandman Papers*, 41–53. Edited by Joe Sanders. Seattle: Fantagraphics Books, 2006.

Buckler, William. *The Victorian Imagination: Essays in Aesthetic Exploration*. New York: New York University, 1980.

Byron, George Gordon, Baron. "Darkness." In *Lord Byron: Selected Poems*, 412–14. Edited by Susan J. Wolfson and Peter J. Manning. New York: Penguin Books, 1996.

Camus, Cyril. "Neil Gaiman: A Portrait of the Artist as a Disciple of Alan Moore." *Studies in Comics*, 2, no. 1 (2011): 147–57. doi:10.1386/stic.2.1.147_1 (accessed October 22, 2021).

Carey, Mike, and Peter Gross, *The Unwritten: Apocalypse*. New York: DC Comics, 2014.

———. *The Unwritten: Leviathan*. New York: DC Comics, 2011.

———. *The Unwritten: On to Genesis*. New York: DC Comics, 2012.

———. *The Unwritten: Tommy Taylor and the Bogus Identity*. New York: DC Comics, 2010.

———. *The Unwritten: Tommy Taylor and the Ship that Sank Twice.* New York: DC Comics, 2014.

———. *The Unwritten: The Wound.* New York: DC Comics, 2013.

Carey, Mike, Peter Gross, and Bill Willingham. *The Unwritten Fables.* New York: DC Comics, 2014.

Carpenter, Greg. *The British Invasion! Alan Moore, Neil Gaiman, Grant Morrison, and the Invention of the Modern Comic Book Writer.* Edwardsville, IL: Sequart Organization, 2016.

Castaldo, Annalisa. "'No More Yielding Than a Dream': The Construction of Shakespeare in *The Sandman.*" *College Literature: A Journal of Critical Literary Studies*, 31, no. 4 (2004): 94–110. doi:10.1353/lit.2004.0052 (accessed October 19, 2021).

Chesterton, G. K. "Ethics of Elfland." In *Orthodoxy*. New York: John Lane Company, 1908. https://archive.org/details/orthodoxy1909ches (accessed October 19, 2021).

———. *Soul of Wit: G. K. Chesterton on William Shakespeare*. Edited by Dale Ahlquist. Mineola, NY: Dover Publications, 2012.

Chute, Hillary. "Comics as Literature? Reading Graphic Narrative," *PMLA*, 123, no. 2 (2008): 452–63. https://www.jstor.org/stable/25501865 (accessed October 22, 2021).

Clark, Susanna. "The Wonderful Wizard of Northampton: *Watchmen* Writer Alan Moore Talks Sex and Superheroes with Novelist Susanna Clark." *The Telegraph*. Last modified October 21, 2019. https://www.telegraph.co.uk/culture/books/authorinterviews/11608804/Susanna-Clark-interviews-Alan-Moore-the-wonderful-wizard-of...-Northampton.html (accessed October 22, 2021).

Coulombe, Charles A. "Hermetic Imagination: The Effect of the Golden Dawn on Fantasy Literature." *Mythlore: A Journal of J. R. R. Tolkien, C. S. Lewis, Charles Williams, and Mythopoeic Literature*, 21, no. 2 (1996): 345–55.

Dan, Joseph, ed. *The Early Kabbalah.* Translated by Ronald Kiener. New York: Paulist Press, 1986.

Derrida, Jacques. "Des Tours de Babel." In *Acts of Religion*, 104–33. Edited by Gil Anidjar. Translated by Joseph F. Graham. New York: Routledge, 2002.

Dowd, Chris. "An Autopsy of Storytelling: Metafiction and Neil Gaiman." In *The Neil Gaiman Reader*, 103–14. Edited by Darrell Schweitzer. Cabin John, MD: Wildside Press, 2007.

The Early Kabbalah. Edited Joseph Dan, Trans. Ronalf Kiener. New York: Paulist Press, 1986.

Gaiman, Neil. "A Speech I Gave Once: On Lewis, Tolkien and Chesterton." Harper Collins Publishers, January 26, 2012. http://journal.neilgaiman.com/2012/01/speech-i-once-gave-on-lewis-tolkien-and.html (accessed October 19, 2021).

———. *Sandman: The Doll's House*. New York: DC Comics, 1990.

———. *Sandman: Dream Country*. New York: DC Comics, 1990.

———. *Sandman: The Kindly Ones*. New York: DC Comics, 2012.

———. *Sandman: Preludes & Nocturnes*. New York: DC Comics, 1988.

———. *Sandman: The Wake*. New York: DC Comics, 1996.

Gordon, Joan. "Prospero Framed in Neil Gaiman's *The Wake*." In *The Sandman Papers*, 79–92. Edited by Joe Sanders. Seattle: Fantagraphics Books, 2006.

Hartman, Geoffrey. "Toward Literary History." *Daedalus*, 99, no. 2, 1970: 355–83. https://www.jstor.org/stable/20023949 (accessed October 22, 2021).

Howell, Tracee. "The Monstrous Alchemy of Alan Moore: *Promethea* as Literacy Narrative." *Studies in the Novel*, 47, no. 3 (2015): 381–98. doi: 10.1353/sdn.2015.0044 (accessed October 22, 2021).

Indick, Ben. "Neil Gaiman in Words and Pictures." In *The Neil Gaiman Reader*, 79–96. Edited by Darrell Schweitzer. Cabin John, MD: Wildside Press, 2007.

Ingleby, Michael. Introduction to *G. K. Chesterton, London, and Modernity*. Edited by Matthew Beaumont and Michael Ingleby, 1–14. New York: Bloomsbury, 2013.

Johnson, Kyle P. "Sequential Narrative in the Shield of Achilles." In *Classics and Comics*, 43–58. Edited by George Kovacs and C. W. Marshall. New York: Oxford University Press, 2011.

Katsiadas, Nick. "Mytho-Auto-Bio: Neil Gaiman's *Sandman*, the Romantics, and Shakespeare's *The Tempest*." *Studies in Comics*, 6, no. 1 (2015): 61–84. doi:10.1386/stic.6.1.61_1 (accessed October 19, 2021).

Katsiadas, Nick. "superheroes as myths," COMIXSCHOLARS-L, University of Florida LISTSERV Archives, April 23, 2018. https://lists.ufl.edu/cgi-bin/wa?A2=COMIXSCHOLARS-L;afc5bc32.1804 (accessed October 25, 2021).

Khoury, George, ed. "Chapter III: The Rising." In *The Extraordinary Works of Alan Moore*, 54–81. Raleigh: TwoMorrows Publishing, 2003.

Kidder, Orion Ussner. "superheroes as myths," COMIXSCHOLARS-L, University of Florida LISTSERV Archives, April 23, 2018. https://lists.ufl.edu/cgi-bin/wa?A2=COMIXSCHOLARS-L;7dc42115.1804

Kovacs, George, and C. W. Marshall, *Classics and Comics*. New York: Oxford University Press, 2011.

Kunzle, David, ed. "Preface." In *Rodolphe Töpffer: The Complete Comic Strips*, ix–xii. Jackson: University of Mississippi Press, 2007.

Landy, Joshua. "Modern Magic: Jean Eugène Robert-Houdin and Stéphane Mallarmé." In *The Re-Enchantment of the World*, 102–29. Edited by Joshua Landy and Michael Saler. Stanford: Stanford University Press, 2009.

Lefèvre, Pascal. "good reference? common mistake of ignoring the visual?" COMIXSCHOLARS-L, University of Florida LISTSERV Archives, January 15, 2019. https://lists.ufl.edu/cgi-bin/wa?A2=COMIXSCHOLARS-L;77f9da8c.1901 (accessed October 25, 2021).

Lynch, Deidre, and Jack Stillinger. "William Blake: 1757–1827." In *The Norton Anthology of English Literature*, 76–79. Edited by Stephen Greenblatt, vol. 2. New York: W. W. Norton & Co., 2006.

Mann, Neil. "The Hermetic Order of the Golden Dawn." *The System of Yeats's* A Vision. Last modified October 29, 2006. http://www.yeatsvision.com/GD.html (accessed October 22, 2021).

McGillis, Roderick. "The Sustaining Paradox: Romanticism and Alan Moore's *Promethea* Novels." In *Time of Beauty, Time of Fear: The Romantic Legacy in the Literature of Childhood*, 200–16. Edited by James Holt McGavran, Jr. Iowa City: University of Iowa Press, 2012. www.jstor.org/stable/j.ctt20q1tn5 (accessed October 18, 2021).

Melville, Herman. *Moby-Dick; or, The Whale*. New York: W. W. Norton & Co., 2018.

Meskin, Aaron. "Comics as Literature?" *British Journal of Aesthetics*, 49, no. 3 (2009): 219–39. doi:10.1093/aesthj/ayp025 (accessed October 22, 2021).

Milbank, Alison. *Chesterton and Tolkien as Theologians: The Fantasy of the Real*. New York: T&T Clark, 2009.

Moore, Alan, and Chris Sprouse. *Tom Strong*. La Jolla: America's Best Comics, 2006.

Moore, Alan, and J. H. Williams III. *Promethea: Book 1*. New York: DC Comics, 2000.

———. *Promethea: Book 2*. New York: DC Comics, 2002.

———. *Promethea: Book 3*. New York: DC Comics, 2002.

———. *Promethea: Book 4*. New York: DC Comics, 2003.

———. *Promethea: Book 5*. New York: DC Comics, 2005.

Murphy, B. Keith. "The Origins of *Sandman*." In *The Sandman Papers*, 3–22. Edited by Joe Sanders. Seattle: Fantagraphics Books, 2006.

Pfau, Thomas. *Romantic Moods: Paranoia, Trauma, and Melancholy, 1790–1840*. Baltimore: Johns Hopkins University Press, 2005.

Rauch, Stephen. *Neil Gaiman's* The Sandman *and Joseph Campbell: In Search of Modern Myth*. Holicong, PA: Wildside Press, 2003.

Reynolds, Richard. *Super Heroes: A Modern Mythology*. Jackson: University Press of Mississippi, 1992.

Ricker, Aaron. "good reference? common mistake of ignoring the visual?" COMIXSCHOLARS-L, University of Florida LISTSERV Archives, January 15, 2019. https://lists.ufl.edu/cgi-bin/wa?A2=COMIXSCHOLARS-L;87cd81ee.1901 (accessed October 18, 2021).

Romagnoli, Alex, and Gian Pagnucci. *Enter the Superheroes: American Values, Culture, and the Canon of Superhero Literature*. Lanham, MD: Scarecrow Press, 2013.

Round, Julia. "Subverting Shakespeare? *The Sandman* #19: 'A Midsummer Night's Dream.'" In *Sub/Versions: Cultural Status, Genre and Critique*, 19–33. Edited by Pauline MacPherson, Christopher Murray, Gordon Spark, and Kevin Corstorphine. Newcastle: Cambridge Scholars Publishing, 2008.

Saler, Michael. *As If: Modern Enchantment and the Literary Prehistory of Virtual Reality*. New York: Oxford University Press, 2012.

Saler, Michael, and Joshua Landy. "Introduction: The Varieties of Modern Enchantment." In *The Re-Enchantment of the World: Secular Magic in a Rational Age*, 1–14. Stanford: Stanford University Press, 2009.

Sanders, Julie. *Adaptation and Appropriation*. New York: Routledge, 2006.

Saunders, Ben. "Divisions in Comics Scholarship," *PMLA*, 124, no. 1 (2009): 292–93. www.jstor.org/stable/25614270 (accessed October 22, 2021).

Saxton, Julie Myers. "Dreams and Fairy Tales: Themes of Rationality and Love in *A Midsummer Night's Dream* and *The Sandman*." In *The Neil Gaiman Reader*, 22–29. Edited by Darrell Schweitzer. Cabin John, MD: Wildside Press, 2007.

Schiller, Friedrich von. *On the Aesthetic Education of Man*. In *The Norton Anthology of Theory and Criticism*, 483–92. Edited by Vincent B. Leitch and William E. Cain. New York: W. W. Norton & Co., 2010.

Shallcross, Michael. *Rethinking G. K. Chesterton and Literary Modernism: Parody, Performance, and Popular Culture*. New York: Routledge, 2018.

Shelley, Percy Bysshe. *Prometheus Unbound: A Lyrical Drama in Four Acts*. In *Romanticism: An Anthology*, 1,138–214. Edited by Duncan Wu. Malden, MA: Blackwell Publishers, 2012.

Varis, Essi. "Something Borrowed: Interfigural Characterization in Anglo-American Fantasy Comics." In *Framescapes: Graphic Narrative Intertexts*, 113–21. Edited by Mikhail Peppas and Sanabelle Ebrahim. Oxford: Inter-Disciplinary Press, 2016.

Vendler, Helen. *Invisible Listeners: Lyric Intimacy in Herbert, Whitman, and Ashbery*. Princeton: Princeton University Press, 2005.

Wandtke, Terrence. *The Comics Scare Returns: The Contemporary Resurgence of Horror Comics*. Rochester, NY: RIT Press, 2018.

Wilkins, Peter. "An Incomplete Project: Graphic Adaptations of *Moby-Dick* and the Ethics of Response." In *Transforming Anthony Trollope: Dispossession, Victorianism and Nineteenth-Century Word and Image*, 217–33. Edited by Simon Grennan and Laurence Grove. Belgium: Leuven University Press, 2015.

Wilson, Edmund. *Axel's Castle: A Study of the Imaginative Literature of 1870–1930*. Edited by Mary Gordon. New York: Farrar, Straus, and Giroux, 1931.

Wolk, Douglas. *Reading Comics: How Graphic Novels Work and What They Mean*. Philadelphia: Da Capo Press, 2007.

Young, James. "The Holocaust as Vicarious Past: Art Spiegelman's *Maus* and the Afterimages of History." *Critical Inquiry*, 24, no. 3 (1998): 666–99.

INDEX

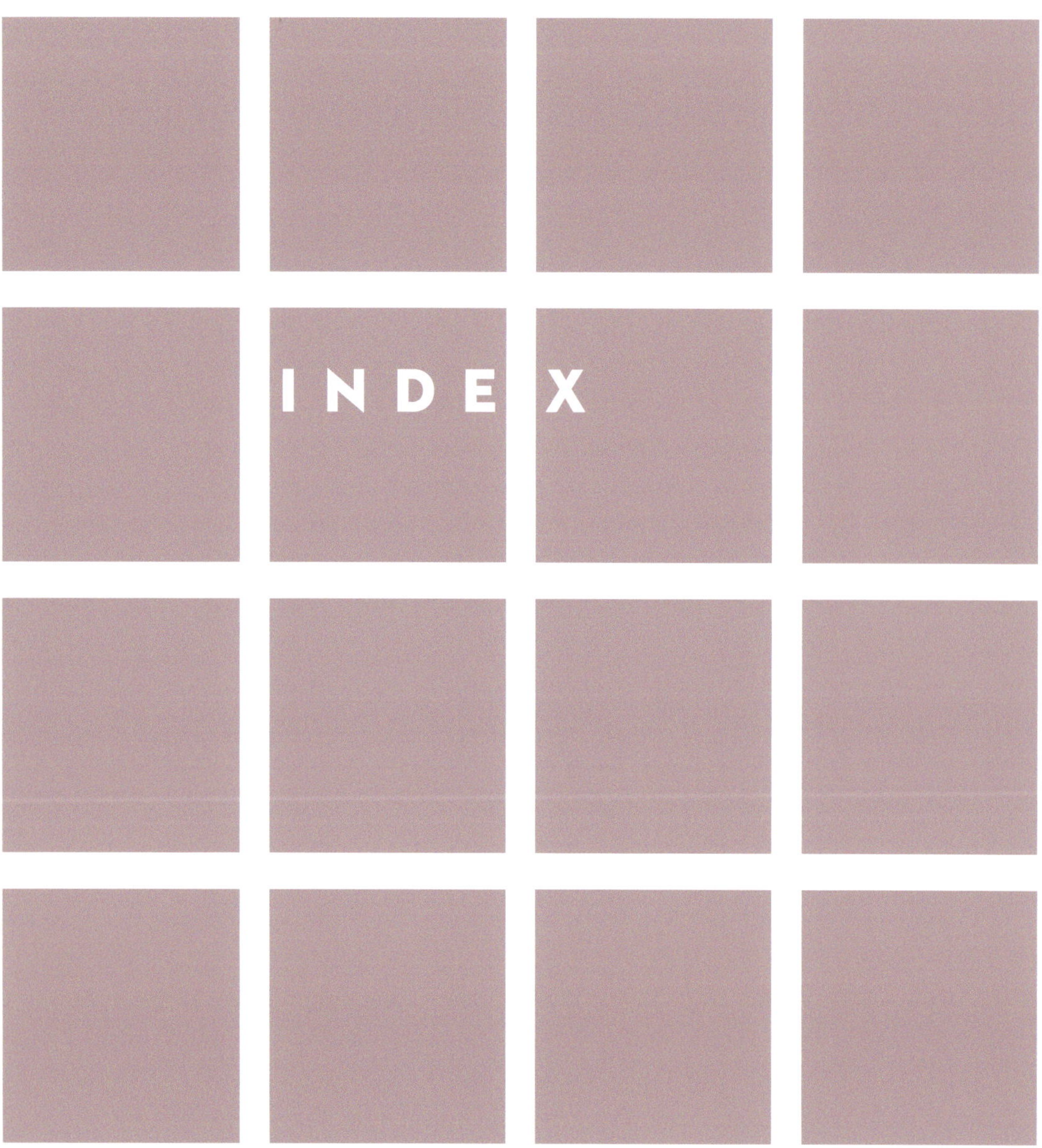

INDEX

COLOPHON

Alexandra Hoff
Editor

Eric. C Wilder
Designer

Frances Chang Andreu
Cover Illustrator

Marnie Soom
Production

More Vang
Alexandria, Virginia
Printer

This book was made possible, in part, through the generosity of More Vang.

Endurance Silk
80 lb. text and 100 lb. cover

Adobe Caslon Pro, Neutraface 2
Typefaces